Janet
Schreiber

7.50

2-1-76

(H)

D0045218

EVALUATIVE RESEARCH

Evaluative Research

PRINCIPLES AND PRACTICE IN PUBLIC

SERVICE & SOCIAL ACTION PROGRAMS

EDWARD A. SUCHMAN, PH.D.

RUSSELL SAGE FOUNDATION

NEW YORK, 1967

Printed March, 1968
Reprinted February, 1969
Reprinted November, 1969
Reprinted June, 1970
Reprinted March, 1971
Reprinted February, 1972
Reprinted April, 1973
Reprinted March, 1974
Reprinted March, 1976

PUBLICATIONS OF RUSSELL SAGE FOUNDATION

Russell Sage Foundation was established in 1907 by Mrs. Russell Sage for the improvement of social and living conditions in the United States. In carrying out its purpose the Foundation conducts research under the direction of members of the staff or in close collaboration with other institutions, and supports programs designed to develop and demonstrate productive working relations between social scientists and other professional groups. As an integral part of its operations, the Foundation from time to time publishes books or pamphlets resulting from these activities. Publication under the imprint of the Foundation does not necessarily imply agreement by the Foundation, its Trustees, or its staff with the interpretations or conclusions of the authors.

RUSSELL SAGE FOUNDATION
230 PARK AVENUE
NEW YORK, N.Y. 10017

Standard Book Number 87154–863–1
Library of Congress Catalog Card Number 67–25913
Printed in the United States of America

CONTENTS

FOREWORD

In these days of large government programs intended to reduce poverty, develop communities, prevent delinquency and crime, control disease, and reconstruct cities, the predominant rhetoric is that of planning, pilot projects, experimental and demonstration programs—and evaluation. Those who seek to select for support the more promising plans and projects submitted to funding agencies have become habituated to the ritualistic inclusion in the proposal of a final section on Evaluation. In most cases this section consists of sometimes grandiose but usually vague statements of intent and procedure for assessing the impact of the proposed action. In some cases there is an elegant, highly academic, and impractical scheme worked out in meticulous detail by an obviously talented research consultant. In a few treasured instances there is a well-considered, realistic, and workmanlike plan for getting some fairly reliable answers to the questions of what worked and why.

Out of all this one gets the impression that what passes for evaluative research is indeed a mixed bag at best and chaos at worst. There are many reasons for this sad state and most of them, strange to say, are nonpejorative, as the present volume makes quite clear. In any case, one reads this book with a sigh of relief and a surge of reviving confidence. So far as this writer is aware, it is the clearest and most comprehensive analysis of the problems and potentialities of evaluative research presently available in the literature.

Dr. Suchman has distilled in this volume a rich and varied research experience, much of it concerned with difficult evaluative problems. While his work in recent years has been in sociological research applied to the problems of public health and education, he has made significant contributions as a research sociologist in many other fields such as consumer behavior, mass communication and public opinion, military training and performance, race and ethnic relations, mental health, and community development. As will be noted, these are areas offering extensive opportunity for applying theory and research methods of social science to practical problems, many of them being problems of determining how and to what extent planned action interventions produce expected—and unexpected—outcomes. There are few issues and perplexities in this field that the author has not encountered, and his treatment of the subject has a ring of authenticity and maturity of judgment that will commend his book to that growing body of administrative and research people confronted by the increasing necessity for reliable assessment of impact of action programs.

This book will have many uses. It will not only provide significant increments of technical knowledge for the evaluative research person, but will aid him in striking a workable balance between rigorous design and method and the situational realities in which he must function. For the operating practitioner whose work is being evaluated, the book should be of material assistance in clarifying what competent evaluation involves and what it can do to improve professional theory and practice.

It is interesting to speculate on the reception this work will have among administrators. These officials are for the most part still skeptical of social science research and its uses in the realm of practical affairs, though there is a growing recognition that policies, plans, and programs addressed to problems of modern life require more and more precise information and understanding of complex social processes. It is my guess that they will find the practical down-to-earth quality of the book coupled with its lucid, unpretentious handling of technical matters of research design and method a welcome aid. The rewarding increase in knowledgeability about the evaluative research process and its potential for program strengthening and innovation should make the work a regular item on the administrator's reference shelf.

Thus far I have stressed the value of Dr. Suchman's book for the world of action. It would be a mistake, however, for the academic scientist to overlook the skillful manner in which the author shows the potentially productive interplay between well-designed and executed evaluative research and the theoretical and methodological developments of the scientific disciplines themselves. For it is in the often frustrating but exciting search for specific causal connections between practical social actions and their consequences that we can expect critical advances in basic social science knowledge.

It is a pleasure indeed to express gratitude to the author for an important task well done.

LEONARD S. COTTRELL, JR.

Russell Sage Foundation
New York, N.Y.
June 30, 1967

ACKNOWLEDGMENTS

This report represents an extension of ideas and materials presented over a three-year period to a seminar on "Evaluation of Public Health Practice" at the Columbia University School of Public Health and Administrative Medicine. Grateful acknowledgment is made to Russell Sage Foundation for support of this seminar and the preparation of the present volume.

Colleagues in the conduct of this seminar and invaluable aides in the development of many of the principles and practices of evaluation discussed in this report were Dr. George James and Dr. Jack Elinson. Indeed, James and Elinson should be recognized as co-authors, in spirit if not in actuality, of this report.

EDWARD A. SUCHMAN

CHAPTER I

An Introduction to Evaluative Research

In recent years there has been a rapidly increasing emphasis upon the utilization of behavioral science concepts and methods for meeting social problems. Partly this is the result of a steady growth in the recognition that "one of the most appealing ideas of our century is the notion that science can be put to work to provide solutions to social problems,"[1] and partly it is a reflection of political circumstances favorable to social action programs. The commitment of first President Kennedy and then President Johnson to the development of "The Great Society" through planned social change has given both societal and financial support to community programs aimed at many different aspects of health, education, and welfare.

SOCIAL CHANGE AND SOCIAL ACTION

We are currently in the midst of a "War on Poverty" which has as its ultimate goal nothing less than the elimination of economic, educational, medical, and social deprivation. Granting the rather difficult and even impractical nature of this goal, not to say its logical inconsistency,[2] there is no denying the surge of activity in these areas and the initiation of domestic and international programs costing billions of dollars. One has only to look at the daily newspaper to find new developments in education, public health, medical care, urban redevelopment, and social welfare. Legislation in all these areas attests to the willingness of Congress to support, even if on occasion with hesitation, these social "reforms." Their public popularity has given rise to increasing citizen pressure for even "bigger and better" programs.

While the major focus of these programs has been overwhelmingly upon action, or the development of operational programs and the delivery of services, the demand that some attempt be made to determine the effectiveness of such public service and social action programs has become increasingly insistent. Social scientists themselves have been growing uneasy about the validity of many of the programs being developed under the umbrella of "applied social science." The result has been a sudden awakening of interest in a long-neglected aspect of social research—the evaluation study. Critics of public service and social action programs in almost all areas have joined the cry for evaluative research. Reviews of programs in such diverse fields as public health,[3] parent education,[4] social casework,[5] mental health,[6] juvenile delinquency,[7] college education,[8] medical care,[9] and adult education,[10] to mention only a few, revealed the paucity of both conceptualization and scientific research on the effectiveness of most activities in these areas.

THE NEED FOR EVALUATION

All social institutions or subsystems, whether medical, educational, religious, economic, or political, are required to provide "proof" of their legitimacy and effectiveness in order to justify society's continued support. Both the demand for and the type of acceptable "proof" will depend largely upon the nature of the relationship between the social institution and the public. In general, a balance will be struck between faith and fact, reflecting the degree of man's respect for authority and tradition within the particular system versus his skepticism and desire for tangible "proofs of work."

It is not difficult to account for the increasing pressures upon public service and community program workers to evaluate their activities. The current desire to judge the worthwhileness of such programs is but one aspect of modern society's belief that many of its social problems can be met most effectively through planned action based upon existing knowledge, including the design of even better solutions in step with advancing knowledge. The commitment of the modern world to planned social change is overwhelmingly apparent on the national and international scene. It is to be found in current approaches to the political, economic, social, and medical problems of the affluent societies and in attempts to change the structure and functioning of the underdeveloped areas.

Underlying this increasing need for evaluation of public service programs are a number of highly significant trends in the nature of social problems, in the structure and functioning of the various fields of public service, and in the needs and expectations of the public. Fundamental changes are taking place in each of these areas and the resulting ferment has created an insistently strong demand for evaluative research to determine the extent to which current programs are meeting the challenge of a rapidly changing world. Let us look at some of these trends briefly for their influence upon both the need for evaluation and the form which such evaluation is taking.

1. *Changes in the Nature of Social Problems.* To a large extent social problems are increasingly being recognized as affecting the entire community and not only the unfortunate victims directly caught up by the problem. This is seen in attempts to shift the label, "The Negro Problem" to "The White Problem," and to make "educational deprivation" a problem for the entire community rather than only for those schools located in poverty areas. In general, this represents a recognition that social institutions rather than individuals bear the major responsibility for the existence of social problems and that institutional reform rather than individual changes in behavior offers the better prospect for attacking these social problems.

To meet this changing definition, new programs of prevention and control are required. Unlike earlier traditional approaches, these programs will only rarely be able to depend on either legislative fiat or executive order, but will require a much greater degree of voluntary public and community cooperation and participation in long-term continuous programs of social change. Mass action by the community at large must replace official services and changes in the social environment will become at least as important as changes in the physical environment.

Evaluation of these programs will require the formulation of new objectives and the development of new criteria of effectiveness. The earlier goals of total problem eradication will have to be forsaken for more realistic goals of improved functioning in the continued presence of long-term social conditions. Systematic early detection and amelioration will largely supplant rehabilitation or "care-taking," while accomplishment will be measured more often in terms of such basic goals as prevention of the problem and of coordination and integration of services in the community.

2. *Changes in the Structure and Function of Public Agencies.* Not only are the goals of public service programs shifting, so is the nature of their organization and operation. The trend is toward broader community participation and responsibility. As a result of the changing social problem picture described above, the dividing line between prevention and treatment is becoming increasingly difficult to determine. In addition, the earlier concentration of public services upon the "needy poor" is giving way to concern with whole segments of the population such as the elderly, infants, and young children, and to broad social problem categories such as the juvenile delinquent and the culturally deprived. These new target

groups have forced official public agencies into a leadership or at least a cooperative role in planning and developing community programs that go far beyond traditional departmental services.

This enlargement of scope and change in the nature of public service activities has created complex problems of organization and resources which demand continuous evaluation and reformulation.[11] New administrative structures, revamped occupational categories, changed educational and training requirements, and increased social services produce new objectives which require a broader type of program evaluation. While one may decry this trend toward greater bureaucratization and specialization, it is inevitable in the growth of our complex, technological society. The task for public and community agencies is to increase the probability of a more efficient and effective organization—a real challenge to program planning, development, and evaluation.

One other aspect of the changing nature of public service and community work that is having a profound effect upon both the quantity and quality of evaluative research is the continued professional growth of the practitioners in the various fields of health, education, and welfare. As public service personnel acquire both advanced training and professional pride in their field of specialization, the demand for self-evaluation and "proof" of the validity of their techniques increases. The tremendous surge in community research is strengthening the scientific basis of public service practice and is adding support to the desire for evaluation of old and new programs.[12] The insistence of the greatly increased governmental sources of funds for program development upon the evaluation of demonstration programs is also forcing a keen and constant awareness of the need to evaluate upon community program research workers.

3. *Changes in the Needs and Expectations of the Public.* As the nature of social problems and the organization of public services have changed, so have the attitudes and behavior of the public both as the targets of public service activity and as the ultimate determiners of the degree and type of support to be given to these programs.[13] In the early days of the public service movement, the obvious health, education, and welfare needs did not require proof of effectiveness. The picture changes radically, however, when one wishes to secure public cooperation for self-help programs or to change individual attitudes and behavior. The need for such programs, on the one hand, and the effectiveness of the proposed remedies, on the other, are much less obvious.

Furthermore, a better-educated and more sophisticated public is less willing than ever to accept the need for community services on faith alone. Increasingly, the public is demanding "scientific" proof of the effectiveness of various programs. To secure the desired voluntary participation of individuals in most current service programs, it will be necessary to document new activities with evidence of their accomplishments. While it may have been sufficient in the early days simply to build facilities and to provide services, it is now necessary to "reach out" to the public with these services in order to secure their greater utilization. "Motivation" is a key problem in community service programs today and one of the primary conditions of motivation is the individual's belief in the effectiveness of the action he is being asked to take.[14,15]

Coupled with this need to be wooed is an increased public expectation of bigger and better services. Such services are becoming defined more as public rights than individual privileges. As a result, the community is taking a more active interest in public matters and exerting a greater influence in the determination of public policy.[16] This has produced an increased pressure upon public agencies for greater accountability. Requests for funds must compete with those of other agencies and new programs must be justified, while old programs are shown to be efficient and effective. In this contest for public support, evaluative research has become a major weapon.[17]

Thus, we see that current changes in each of three major aspects of public service and community action—(a) the social problem; (b) the service agencies; and (c) the public—reinforce each other to produce a growing demand for evaluative research. This need will become even more intense in the near future. These trends are just beginning and all the pressures in the field are pushing toward an increasingly important role for evaluative research.

There can be little doubt about the new directions in which public services are moving today. But new directions are almost always accompanied by basic, if disturbing, questions concerning the most desirable means and ends. These questions are, to a large extent, the basis for the currently increasing interest in the evaluation of modern public service programs. There probably comes a time in the growth of any new field when, after the initial outburst of enthusiastic activity, a breathing period of evaluation sets in. During this stage, there is likely to be a demand for careful appraisals of old and new programs—research studies designed to test the relative worth of the longstanding, established activities as compared to the new or proposed programs.

Health, education, and welfare programs at the present time are experiencing undeniable pressures for such a period of evaluation. These pressures are healthy insofar as they force a rapidly expanding field to balance the excitement of new discoveries with the hardheaded realities of succussful application. These pressures are further enhanced by a combination of expanding knowledge and constricting budgets. If the public services are to move successfully toward new programs based upon new knowledge, they must be prepared to justify such new programs in the constant battle for funds—a battle in which the old, established programs have the advantage of traditional support from both administrative groups and a public which has become accustomed to such services.

Research, it would appear, helps to set the stage for this type of battle between the old and the new. It may be expected that increased research will usually result in new knowledge which, in turn, will often create the need for new programs that, unfortunately, usually require additional funds. This conflict between the old and the new demands well-designed evaluation studies for its most desirable resolution.

Thus, the current period of expanding knowledge and tightened budgets in the field of public service is "ripe" for the advancement of evaluative research. For several years in a row, budget directors in most cities have fought requests for money for new and expanded public services. This conflict undoubtedly will become worse rather than better in the immediate future. Therefore, if new knowledge in health, education, and welfare is to find its way into new programs, current activities must be evaluated to determine what reallocation of resources can take place, while new activities must be carefully pretested and evaluated before they are put into practice.

This growing demand for evaluation constitutes the rationale for this report. Unfortunately, the theory and method of evaluative research have lagged far behind the development of the scientific methodology of nonevaluative research. Today, as modern man turns more and more to basic research for his answers to practical problems, a great need exists for the methodological development of evaluative research as a reliable and valid means of testing the degree to which scientific knowledge is being successfully put to practical use. To as large an extent as possible, the same rigorous criteria that were used to develop knowledge must also be used to test the application of that knowledge.

Almost all fields of applied knowledge are concerned with this problem of evaluation. Conferences and discussions during the past few years on evaluation in different public service areas have revealed a great many diverse ideas and uneven examples of major and minor attempts at evaluation. Without exception, summaries of these conferences have concluded that there is a definite need for a careful appraisal of the principles and methods of evaluation itself as applied to public service programs. The wide range of existing evaluation studies needs systematic classification according to significant criteria of content and method. There are many types and levels of evaluation, and it is to be hoped that a careful analysis of the underlying components, in terms of both means and ends, will result in a more meaningful definition of evaluation and a more useful system for classifying, comparing, and making more cumulative the many evaluation studies, past, present, and future.

Many basic questions in the field of evaluation require careful consideration before order can be achieved. We need to know more about the assumptions under which evaluation operates. We need to know more about the purposes and goals of the evaluation study. Methodology for the conduct of evaluative research requires careful analysis and formulation, especially in the light of new developments in social research. Many of the newer techniques and research designs, such as motivational and operations research, have not yet been adequately incorporated into the planning and conduct of evaluation studies. The valid interpretation and successful application of findings, while the *sine qua non* of evaluation, is often grossly neglected and misunderstood. These are only some of the important problems and needs in the field of evaluation. Undoubtedly one of the reasons that many of the current attempts at evaluation have seemed weak and invalid is the lack of any clear-cut theory or method to support the research.

In our approach, we will make a distinction between "evaluation" and "evaluative research." The former will be used in a general way as referring to the social process of making judgments of worth. This process is basic to almost all forms of social behavior, whether that of a single individual or a complex organization. While it implies some logical or rational basis for making such judgments, it does not require any systematic procedures for marshaling and presenting objective evidence to support the judgment. Thus, we retain the term "evaluation" in its more common-sense usage as referring to the general process of assessment or appraisal of value.

"Evaluative research," on the other hand, will be restricted to the utilization of scientific research methods and techniques for the purpose of making an evaluation. In this sense, "evaluative" becomes an adjective specifying a type of research. The major emphasis is upon the noun "research," and evaluative research refers to those procedures for collecting and analyzing data which increase the possibility for "proving" rather than "asserting" the worth of some social activity. This is not to deny the tremendous social significance of the latter, but only to propose the application of empirical research techniques, insofar as they have been developed in the social sciences today, to the process of evaluation. Our task, in part, will be to evaluate the desirability and feasibility of utilizing such social research methods for the purpose of evaluation. In Chapter III we will expand upon the conceptual, methodological, and operational differences between evaluative and nonevaluative research. For the present, we wish only to explain our distinction between "evaluation," as referring to the general process of evaluating regardless of the type of "evaluation study" made, and "evaluative research," as referring to the utilization of empirical social research methodology for the purposes of conducting such evaluation studies.

In general, this report will deal with the conceptual, methodological, and administrative aspects of evaluation applied to public service and social action programs. We conceive of these programs in a very broad sense. We have not attempted a rigorous definition of public service or social action, but include any organized effort on the part of some official or voluntary agency to provide some public service or to meet some social problem. Our emphasis is upon evaluative research as a method for studying the effectiveness of such efforts at planned social change. While we have tried to frame the presentation in such a way as to apply to public service programs in general, most of the examples will be drawn from the field of public health. This is the area in which the author has had the most experience and around which the materials were originally collected.

The book is divided into three main sections, representing the conceptual, the methodological, and the administrative aspects of evaluation. We begin with a brief, historical account of evaluative research and a general critique of the current status of evaluation studies, with particular emphasis upon the shortcomings of many of the evaluation guides proposed for community self-surveys of public service programs (Chapter II). This introduction is followed by a conceptual analysis of the evaluation process, including a definition of evaluative research and the place of values, objectives, and assumptions in such research (Chapter III), and concluding with an analysis of different levels of objectives and categories of evaluation (Chapter IV).

The next three chapters deal with methodological problems in evaluative research. We begin by comparing evaluative with nonevaluative research, summarizing different approaches to evaluation, and discussing the formulation of an evaluative research problem (Chapter V). An analysis of various research designs applicable to evaluative research is presented in the following chapter, with detailed emphasis being given to the three main conditions of an evaluative research design: (1) sampling equivalent experimental and control groups, (2) isolation and control of the stimulus, and (3) definition and measurement of the criteria of effect (Chapter VI). The final chapter on methodology takes up the problems of reliability, validity, and differential results in the measurement of the effects of a program (Chapter VII).

Administrative aspects of evaluation are discussed next; first, the place of evaluation in the administrative process as related to program planning, demonstration, and operation, including an analysis of administrative resistance and barriers to evaluation (Chapter VIII); and second, problems in the administration of evaluation studies, such as resources, role relationships, the carrying-out of an evaluation study, and the utilization (or nonutilization) of the findings (Chapter IX).

The book concludes with a brief exposition on the relationship of evaluative research to social experimentation, stressing the potential contribution which public service and social action programs can make to our knowledge of administrative science and social change (Chapter X).

NOTES TO CHAPTER I

1. Zetterberg, Hans L., *Social Theory and Social Practice*. The Bedminster Press, Totowa, N.J., 1962, p. 15.
2. Suchman, Edward A., "Medical Deprivation," *American Journal of Orthopsychiatry*, vol. 36, July, 1966, pp. 665–672.
3. Ennes, Howard, editor, *A Critique of Community Public Health Services*, American Journal of Public Health, vol. 47, part 2, November, 1957. (Entire issue.)
4. Brim, Orville G., Jr., *Education for Child Rearing*. Russell Sage Foundation, New York, 1959.
5. Breedlove, J. L., and M. S. Krause, "Evaluative Research Design: A Social Casework Illustration," in Gottschalk, L. A., and A. H. Auerback, editors, *Methods of Research in Psychotherapy*. Appleton-Century-Crofts, New York, 1966, pp. 456–477.

6. *Evaluation in Mental Health,* U.S. Department of Health, Education, and Welfare, Public Health Service, Publication No. 413, Government Printing Office, Washington, 1955.
7. Witmer, Helen L., and E. Tufts, *The Effectiveness of Delinquency Prevention Programs.* Children's Bureau, Publication No. 340, Washington, 1954.
8. Jacob, Phillip E., *Changing Values in College,* Harper and Bros., New York, 1957; Barton, Allen H., *Studying the Effects of College Education,* The Edward H. Hazen Foundation, New Haven, 1959.
9. Donabedian, Avedis, "Evaluating the Quality of Medical Care," *Milbank Memorial Fund Quarterly,* vol. 44, part 2, July, 1966, pp. 166–203.
10. Wilder, David E., "Problems of Evaluation Research," in Brunner, Edmund de S., and others, editors, *An Overview of Adult Education Research.* Adult Education Association, Chicago, 1959, p. 272.
11. Dixon, James P., "Developing Problems of Official Services in Keeping with the Times," *American Journal of Public Health,* vol. 47, part 2, November, 1957, pp. 15–19.
12. James describes this new responsibility as applied to the public health officer as follows: "Instead of simply administering his department in keeping with a pattern of appropriate programs meeting approved standards, he must develop it by means of proper scientific methods so as to keep his programs effective, timely, and streamlined," James, George, "Research by Local Health Departments—Problems, Methods, Results," *American Journal of Public Health,* vol. 48, March, 1958, p. 360.
13. Koos, Earl L., "New Concepts in Community Organization for Health," *American Journal of Public Health,* vol. 43, April, 1953, pp. 468–469.
14. Rosenstock, Irwin, and others, *The Impact of Asian Influenza on Community Life.* U.S. Public Health Service, Publication No. 766, Government Printing Office, Washington, 1960.
15. Hochbaum, Godfrey M., *Public Participation in Medical Screening Programs.* U.S. Public Health Service, Publication No. 572, Government Printing Office, Washington, 1958.
16. Sanders, Irwin T., "Public Health in the Community," in Freeman, Howard, Sol Levine, and Leo G. Reeder, editors, *Handbook of Medical Sociology.* Prentice-Hall, Inc., Englewood Cliffs, N.J., 1963, pp. 369–396.
17. Weisbrod, Burton A., "Does Better Health Pay?" *Public Health Reports,* vol. 75, June, 1960, pp. 557–560.

CHAPTER II

The Growth and Current Status
of Evaluation

Man's need to know is closely coupled with his wish to judge. The natural curiosity which leads man to ask the question "Why?" also underlies his drive to discover "Cui bono?" or "What good is it?" Concern with the good or evil consequences of man's attempts to control his environment has marked the history of new discoveries and their application. Evaluation of utility is intrinsically interwoven with the development of knowledge. While the ideal norms of science may stress objectivity and a disinterest in practical significance, the conduct and support of scientific research only rarely escapes the more operational norms of an evaluation of "Knowledge for What?"[1]

An evaluation is basically a judgment of worth—an appraisal of value. The object being appraised may be a tangible piece of property whose value is counted in dollars and cents, a human being whose goodness is judged according to his virtues or vices, an activity or program whose success is measured by the results it achieves, or even a whole social system or parts of that system whose functioning may be evaluated in terms of smoothness of operation or conflict.[2] In short, all objects or actions have value and descriptions of such objects or acts usually contain some affective judgment about this value. Thus, in many respects, to think about something is often to evaluate it in some way. Everyday language is full of descriptive adjectives connoting value and judgment, such as beautiful, wise, useless, bad.

The process of evaluating is highly complex and subjective. Inherently it involves a combination of basic assumptions underlying the activity being evaluated and of personal values on the part of both those whose activities are being evaluated and those who are doing the evaluation. Evaluation is a continuous social process, rarely stopping to challenge these assumptions or to bring the values into the open. The task for the development of evaluative research as a "scientific" process is to "control" this intrinsic subjectivity, since it cannot be eliminated.

This brief introduction to the problem highlights the primary nature of our task. We propose to examine the principles and procedures that man has developed for controlling subjectivity—the scientific method—for their applicability to the social process of evaluation and, on the basis of some general understanding of the extent to which this is possible, to describe and analyze current evaluative research for those factors which promote or deter the achievement of this goal. Thus, from the beginning, we would like to make it clear that we do not view the field of evaluation as having any methodology different from the scientific method; evaluative research is, first and foremost, *research* and as such must adhere as closely as possible to currently accepted standards of research methodology. While the purposes or objectives of evaluation may favor variations of research design, and while administrative conditions may require adaptations of research technique, ultimately the significance of the results must be determined according to the same scientific standards used to judge non-evaluative research.

The extent to which these standards are met even in basic research, however, is a relative matter subject to a great deal of "slippage" depending upon norms of feasibility rather than unequivocal rules. Some studies do come closer to the ideal than others—and this can be taken as the guiding "value" in this analysis of the evaluation process—some evaluation studies are better than others (even granting the fact that many are patently "bad")[3]—but why? And what can be done to raise the ratio of better to worse?

BACKGROUND OF EVALUATIVE RESEARCH

From their early beginnings, the various fields of public service have been concerned with proving the effectiveness of their programs. Engaged in community activities dependent upon public support and utilizing knowledge derived from basic scientific disciplines, the various professionals involved in public service programs have often felt (if not whole-heartedly accepted) the responsibility to "prove" their claims. At no time has this been more true than today. The literature abounds with reports of evaluation studies and with discussions on the place of evaluation in public service.[4] A survey of 50 national and state health officials dealing with current public health needs ranked evaluation among the three most important tasks facing community health services today.[5]

It is not suprising that one finds the growth and development of evaluative research in public service closely paralleling the history of the public service movement itself. This history reflects a combination of the three major factors discussed previously: (1) the nature of the dominant social problems of the time; (2) the current form of administrative organization for public service; and (3) the structure and functioning of society, including prevalent social values. Of less importance, but still significant, are the state of knowledge concerning the problem and available techniques and facilities for prevention and service. In regard to evaluation itself, the existing state of knowledge concerning the principles and procedures of evaluative research would also affect the quantity and quality of evaluation, although this relationship is not often recognized or discussed.

Looking briefly at the major eras of public service development, we find first, an early period of authority, marked by reliance upon a "benevolent despotism" for the existence of public services. It is probably true that even such early public services were supported by empirical, trial-and-error "evaluations" which developed a valid body of operational procedures even in the absence of knowledge of underlying processes. Such evaluations undoubtedly were stacked in favor of the existing autocratic officials, but the fact remains that, even during this era of authority, the need for demonstrating success to the public was present to some degree.

With the advent of the period of revolution and enlightenment in the eighteenth century, public service entered an era of research, experimentation, and extended program development. For a period of almost 200 years, beginning slowly but reaching a climax in our present century, public service administration offered to the public a choice of preventive and service programs based increasingly upon "scientific" evaluations of their effectiveness. In the field of public health, for example, vital statistics and morbidity and mortality data offered the first possibility of an objective measurement of the state of health of a nation. Graunt (1662) and Holley (1693), as precursors to the modern public health statistician, proposed the use of these rates for overall governmental planning of public services.[6]

In the field of public health, pioneers like Lemuel Shattuck, Edwin Chadwick, John Howard, and C. E. A. Winslow sparked a drive to undertake community health programs, to establish official public health departments, and to initiate health surveys for the collection of data in order to evaluate the effectiveness of these activities in lowering morbidity and mortality. In 1874 the American Public Health Association, immediately following its formation, appointed a committee "to prepare schedules for the purpose of collecting information with regard to the present condition of public hygiene in the principal towns and cities of the United States."[7] Then followed a period of mounting health surveys and program evaluations—Haven Emerson refers to nearly 600 community health surveys made from 1907 to 1927.[8] Here, indeed, was an era of statistical bookkeeping related to a public service.

However, statistical indices were not enough. Although such measures described the state of current conditions and the number and kinds of activities that were being carried on, they did not permit any specific evaluation of how well or poorly a public service or community agency was doing. The demand shifted to comparative ratings of communities. In 1914 Charles V. Chapin developed a series of rating sheets "of value in pointing out the weak points in each state by the strengthening of which the relative standing of the state may be revised."[9]

These various Community Appraisal Forms, Evaluation Schedules, Grading Standards, and Guides to a Community Self-Survey[10] had as their main characteristics: (1) content based on group judgment of experts throughout the United States; (2) a selective array of subject matter regarded as most important in evaluating local programs; (3) a method of scoring or rating the degree of achievement; and (4) ratings based on actual services rendered as well as funds and personnel.[11]

It must be remembered that the period during which these evaluation schedules were being developed was one of intense public service activity in the fields of health, education, and welfare. The accent was upon program development, upon the initiation of new services to meet obvious demands, and upon the building of facilities to serve the rapidly increasing public need. The immediate job took up everyone's time. Service, rather than research or evaluation, was the keynote of public agencies. It is not surprising that the priority of evaluation ran well behind that given to the administration of the program itself. So great was the faith in service techniques that public agency and community workers usually begrudged any diversion of effort or funds away from them. For example, when the handicapped children's programs achieved nationwide attention, the cry was for more clinics, more children brought to care, more programs offering corrective services. Not one carefully planned, controlled, prospective evaluation study of the long-range restorative power of these programs was begun.

It was not until after World War I that any real demand for critical self-appraisal set in. Rapidly expanding services were producing a degree of chaos which demanded some attempt at uniformity and the establishment of standards if public service was to advance as a professional field. The major purpose of the resulting, rather arbitrary, evaluation guides was to increase standardization and to provide some incentive for meeting these established standards. Appraisal forms were sent periodically to local officials, asking them to make a self-evaluation of their activities. These appraisal forms served two positive functions: (a) they informed the officials of what the standards were; and (b) they provided models for record-keeping. Honor rolls and citations were often used to reward those communities meeting certain standards.

Any critical review of these efforts to produce useful evaluation guides should keep in mind this historical perspective. As public services became more securely established in the community, as community workers matured professionally, and as social and administrative research added a more basic understanding of community processes, much of the justification and many of the underlying assumptions of these standards have come into question. The diminishing use of these community appraisal forms and the difficulties and general failure of most recent attempts to revise these evaluation guides attests to the fact that they are now largely out-of-date. But, *during their time,* these efforts at evaluation served the very useful function of building an awareness of the need for standards against which public service activities could be judged and of creating within public service workers an increasing appreciation of the importance, and difficulties, of evaluative research. There can be little doubt that this growing concern with evaluation did much to raise the general level of public service activity throughout the country and to advance the standing of public service workers as a profession.[12]

A CRITIQUE OF EVALUATION GUIDES

It will be instructive for the purposes of this report on evaluation to review briefly the main weaknesses and shortcomings of this approach to evaluation through the use of self-rating appraisal forms. These criticisms may serve as our initial statement of what evaluation is and what it must do. To begin with, it is interesting to note the principles of evaluation set forth by Sydenstricker as far back as 1926:[13]

1. Specific activities, rather than the program as a whole, should be measured first. (p. 15)
2. The objectives and methods of a public health effort should be clearly defined. (p. 16)
3. Principles of experimentation should be applied. (p. 18)

4. The use of "experimental" and "control" groups or areas should be
   followed. (p. 20)

These basic requirements of evaluative research were largely ignored in
the development of appraisal guides and indices, probably not so much
from a lack of awareness of their importance as from the strong pressure
to produce an instrument which appeared at least administratively feasible. As we shall discuss later, one of the key elements in evaluative research is a productive compromise between methodological requirements
and administrative limitations. In the case of the early evaluation guides
perhaps too great an emphasis was placed upon administrative as compared to scientific considerations.

The shortcomings of these evaluation guides—and, it should be pointed
out, of a great deal of evaluative research in general—may be classified according to: (1) subject matter or objectives, (2) methodology or procedures, and (3) personnel or administration.[14] We will only summarize
these criticisms briefly here, since each area constitutes the focus for a
separate chapter to follow. In large measure, this summary constitutes a
preview of the problems to be discussed in the remainder of this book.

1. *Subject Matter or Objectives*

(a) The arbitrary selection of problems and services tends to stress
traditional activities at the expense of newly developing areas.

(b) The emphasis upon resources and facilities tends to neglect the effectiveness of these activities. Countable activities become substituted for
achievement. Thus, the evaluation becomes one of amount of effort expended rather than the actual outcome.

(c) The accent on quantity of services or activities results in a disregard for measures of the quality of these services. This quantitative bias
tends to result in record-keeping just for the sake of counting and not for
evaluation.

(d) Too many of the program objectives are based upon largely untested or even unsound assumptions whose validity rests primarily upon
tradition or common sense and not on proven effectiveness.

(e) The confusion between levels of objectives and the failure to consider the interrelationships between different functional levels of organization often produces a mixture of ultimate, intermediate, and immediate
objectives.

(f) The objectives given and the standards proposed often represent
ideal rather than realistic goals. While these standards set a mark toward

which a worker can strive, in the absence of any consideration of what is possible or feasible, these standards may be discouraging and thus defeat their purpose. There is the additional danger that, once established, these standards tend to become frozen and difficult to revise in keeping with changing conditions.

2. *Method of Procedure*

(a) The primary reliance of the evaluation guides upon existing records discourages the utilization of research for the collection and analysis of data. This means that in most cases one deals with statistics obtained from samples of biased or unknown representativeness, with available rather than pertinent data, with unreliable and invalid measures, and with relationships whose causal connections are not at all clear.

(b) The absence of any "experimental" design usually results in the lack of any "control" or comparison group. This makes it extremely difficult to determine whether any observable change or improvement can be attributed to the influence of the activity. Many other factors besides an agency's programs are at work in a community and, lacking any control measures, one cannot know to what extent changing indices represent successful or unsuccessful agency activities.

(c) The measurement of the various indices and the rates and ratios computed are of unknown accuracy and reliability. Very little confidence can be placed on the preciseness of the index or on a similar result being obtained upon repetition—if, indeed, repetition is ever provided for. Thus, the significance of changes over time or of comparisons with other communities becomes a highly risky matter.

(d) The standards and weights used to compute the "goodness" of an activity are highly subjective and arbitrary. The number of points given each activity, and, in fact, the choice of the activity itself are based on authority and expert judgment and not on any objective, verifiable criteria. These standards and weights usually represent current practice in the better organized, more affluent communities and may not be applicable to many other communities.

(e) The large differences between communities in the United States makes cross-comparisons of doubtful utility. Little allowance is made in the ratings for specific local conditions. Size of community, geographical location, availability of funds and resources, and so on make the interpretation of differences among communities extremely difficult.

(f) The emphasis upon descriptive statistics and the lack of concern with causal relationships produce a large array of facts with little possibil-ity of meaningful interpretation. The causal nexus between activity and process is rarely investigated. Thus, variations in these evaluations become extremely difficult to explain and, in turn, contribute little or nothing to the advancement of knowledge.

3. Administration

(a) The evaluation guides are prepared mainly for service personnel who have neither the training, skills, nor experience for evaluative re-search. The result is that both the collection and interpretation of data are highly unsophisticated and suffer from a lack of scientific rigor. Further-more, the unevenness with which scientific standards are applied by the different program personnel makes comparisons of ratings highly ques-tionable—often at the penalty of the more rigorous research worker.

(b) The fact that the guides represent self-evaluations subjects them to an almost inevitable personal bias. It is extremely difficult to see one's own program objectively, especially when the results of the appraisal are being used to judge one's performance relative to others.

(c) The need to carry out these evaluations, for the most part, during and in addition to one's usual service activities rarely permits the alloca-tion of sufficient time for planning, data collection, and analysis. The lack of sufficient time, money, and personnel for program evaluation serves only to lower the quality of such evaluative research.

This listing of the shortcomings of various attempts at the preparation of evaluation guides highlights the theoretical, methodological, and ad-ministrative needs of evaluative research in general. These deficiencies be-come increasingly apparent as public service moves from a problem to a community orientation.[15]

A broadened definition of public service as including the positive well-being of the individual and not simply the absence of undesirable social conditions[16] has meant that service agencies have become involved in many community activities which are less directly related to amelioration and more concerned with the prevention of social problems such as cul-tural deprivation, rehabilitation of the indigent, juvenile delinquency, and urban redevelopment, to mention a few.[17] Increasingly, public service workers are called upon to work with community forces as well as specific clients. These trends and the needs for community services, including the development of appropriate evaluation techniques, are areas of growing concern in the field of public service administration.

This, then, is the current state of affairs, in general, of "official" attempts at evaluation in public service. The obvious need is for a critical reevaluation of both the role and the methods of evaluative research in the fields of public service and social action. This is the primary objective of the present report. There has been a gradual shift in the emphasis of evaluation studies away from the use of general appraisal guides to the setting up of carefully planned evaluative research of specific services and objectives and closely tied into program planning and development. This approach with its emphasis upon evaluation as a research procedure utilizing the scientific method for the collection and analysis of data is the basic rationale of the chapters to follow.

Increasing recognition is being given to this need to provide a methodologically sound framework for evaluative research. Knutson has pointed out the importance of defining one's objectives more specifically in terms of a hierarchy of objectives and the determination and evaluation of the intervening conditions that are necessary for the achievement of the ultimate objective.[18] Ciocco has stressed the importance of working with indices of known reliability and validity and of viewing evaluation as a research process.[19] Fleck, in an analysis of the logical basis for evaluation, points out the importance of the personal bias involved in self-evaluation and the need for "professional" evaluation by experienced, objective research workers.[20] The use of the basic experimental research design for evaluation purposes is discussed by Greenberg and Mattison, who again emphasize the fact that evaluative research is after all research and, to be meaningful, it must conform to the basic tenets of research methodology.[21]

CURRENT PROBLEMS OF EVALUATIVE RESEARCH

Given this background of the development of evaluation of public service programs and this brief statement of what evaluative research should and could be, what can we say about the current status of evaluation? Where do public service and social action programs stand today in regard to evaluating the effectiveness of their efforts? What are some of the major problems they are facing in their current attempts at evaluation?

Most critiques of evaluative research today conclude that too few evaluation studies are being made and that, furthermore, those that do exist are generally of low quality. The overwhelming proportion of established public service activities, it is claimed, are not based upon and do not provide for an evaluation of their effectiveness, while most new programs fail to include a plan for evaluation in their development.[22] In general, we concur with these criticisms. Although there are notable exceptions, most of what passes for evaluative research in most fields of public service, such as health, social work, and education, is very poor indeed. What is wrong? Why? And what can be done about it?

The frequency of exhortations to "do better" evaluative research in the literature is closely matched by a sympathetic awareness of the difficulty of obeying this edict. Thus, James consoles his colleagues, "Let there be no mistake about the difficulties in carrying out evaluation research,"[23] while a report from the Public Health Service elaborates, "Evaluation of mental health activities is necessarily difficult. It must cope with the influences of numerous variables, consider the validity of those basic assumptions upon which mental health relies at the present time, and take into account the personal beliefs and attitudes of both the evaluators and those whose activities are being evaluated."[24] Unfortunately, few of these discussions of evaluation attempt to analyze the source of those difficulties or to set forth guiding principles or procedures to help lessen if not overcome some of the problems. In general, the wide range of variation in what is labeled "evaluation," the lack of any clear-cut definition of either the objectives or procedures of evaluative research, the myriad of uses to which evaluation studies are put only serve to make even more troublesome what is inherently a difficult task. These are all important problems which we shall discuss in detail in the chapters to follow.

As we have stated previously, and as will be demonstrated in the chapters on methodology, evaluative research represents an attempt to utilize the scientific method for the purpose of assessing the worthwhileness of an activity. In its research design and its procedures for collecting and analyzing data, it must attempt to adhere as closely as possible to the canons of the scientific method.[25] The same procedures that were used to discover knowledge are now being called upon to evaluate one's ability to apply this knowledge. By adopting the scientific method, the hope is that the results of the evaluation study will be more objective and of ascertainable reliability and validity.

There can be no doubt that the more one can satisfy the rules of scientific method in designing and carrying out one's evaluation study, the more confidence one can place on the objectivity of one's findings. Nevertheless, it is essential to remember that basic research has a different purpose from evaluative research. The next chapter will discuss this and other differences between evaluative and other kinds of research in more detail. The primary objective of basic research is the discovery of knowledge, the proof or disproof of a hypothesis. No administrative action is usually contemplated or need follow. Therefore, the major criterion of the "success" of a basic research project is the scientific validity of its findings, inherently involving an evaluation against the rules of scientific methodology.

But evaluative research is generally applied or administrative research, the primary objective of which is to determine the extent to which a given program or procedure is achieving some desired result. The "success" of an evaluation project will be largely dependent upon its usefulness to the administrator in improving services. Thus, while scientific criteria may determine the degree of confidence one may place on the findings of an evaluation study, administrative criteria will play an even larger role in determining the worthwhileness of the study having been done. Unlike the basic researcher, the applied researcher must be constantly aware of the potential utility of his findings. Only rarely can he take consolation in the fact that "the operation was a success but the patient died."

This, then, is what makes evaluative research "difficult." In theory, the research design problems are often simpler than for nonevaluative research. "Hypotheses" are largely given by the stated objectives and procedures of the program or service being evaluated (although, as we shall see later, in practice, the statement of program objectives and procedures raises significant problems for the evaluator). Furthermore, the research design almost always attempts to conform to the experimental model of before-and-after measurements of an experimental and control group (although here, too, several adaptations are available to the research worker). Perhaps one of the easiest of research assignments is to lay out an "ideal" evaluation study design.

It is not so much the principles of research that make evaluation studies difficult, but rather the practical problems of adhering to these principles in the face of administrative considerations. To a far greater extent than the basic researcher, the evaluator loses control over the research situation. Someone else, usually a program administrator with a strong vested interest, has already defined the objectives of the program to be evaluated. To force him to question the underlying assumptions of these objectives is both difficult and painful. To subdivide these objectives further in terms of intermediate steps toward some ultimate objective often appears to the program administrator as an attempt to limit or destroy his program. Introducing the criterion of performance instead of effort and of efficiency as well as effectiveness seems to question his competence. The presence of this biased third party between the evaluator and the object of his research creates largely unavoidable difficulties usually not faced by the basic researcher.

Add to this natural suspicion and antagonism of the program administrator the fact that most evaluation studies require some degree of interference with ongoing activities and there is further reason for objection and unwilling cooperation. The evaluator does not usually limit himself to observation and measurement as does the basic researcher; he must often ask that procedures be altered somewhat or services withheld completely in order to secure some form of control or comparative group. He may require the keeping of extra records or the securing of additional information not necessary for the operation of the program but essential for the purposes of evaluation. And all this, to be meaningful, must usually be done in the course of the ongoing, day-to-day operation of the program. It makes limited sense in an evaluation study to set up an artificial experimental situation.

The need from the administrator's point of view is for the evaluation to be "simple and practical," at the same time that the methodological requirements of evaluative research move increasingly toward the complex and specialized. As we shall indicate in the chapters on the administrative aspects of evaluation, a balance must be attained between the administrative limitations and the methodological requirements of evaluative research. Not all evaluation studies require the same degree of scientific rigor and many administrative decisions can be made on the basis of limited evaluations. The need for the future is a greater understanding of the different forms that evaluation can take and when each is appropriate.

Finally, evaluation today suffers from a general lack of funds, facilities, time, and personnel. Public service and community action agencies are busily engaged in setting up programs to meet the obvious needs of the community. Most of these programs have face validity and seldom seem to require evaluative research to prove their effectiveness. Only recently, as a result of the trends discussed previously, has evaluative research been given a higher priority. But as compared to the provision of services, and even to basic research, the amount of time, money, and people allocated to evaluation is woefully inadequate. Evaluative research, like all research, costs money and can no more be made an extracurricular or part-time activity of service personnel than can basic research. While certain record collecting procedures can be introduced into ongoing services to provide elementary data on evaluation, these procedures can rarely provide valid program evaluations. Trained research personnel working with special evaluation funds are the *sine qua non* of any movement toward "scientific" evaluative research. Unless this basic requirement is met, it is doubtful that evaluative research in the future will be any better than it has been in the past.

The question may legitimately be raised as to whether the field of evaluative research today is ready to assume a more significant role. Certainly there is a paucity of critical analysis of the proper place of evaluation and an even greater dearth of methodological discussion on the kinds of adaptations of research design most conducive to productive evaluation studies. It is difficult to say which is the chicken and which is the egg. Is evaluative research so neglected today because we don't know enough to make good evaluation studies or haven't we learned enough because it is so neglected? It is our conviction that evaluation today suffers from the lack of any systematic analysis of the theoretical, methodological, and administrative principles underlying its objectives and procedures. We believe that one of the major reasons for its current state of abuse and disrepute is the absence of guidelines and standards for the conduct of evaluation studies. It is our hope that this report will at least open the door to further debate and analysis of the functions, objectives, and methods of evaluative research.

NOTES TO CHAPTER II

1. For a general discussion of the problem, see Lynd, Robert S., *Knowledge for What?* Princeton University Press, Princeton, N.J., 1939. As stated editorially by the *American Journal of Public Health* in welcoming the First National Conference on Evaluation in Public Health, "Consciously or subconsciously evaluation is an inseparable part of human life and one of the characteristics that distinguishes the behavior of the cerebrating *homo sapiens* from the instinct-guided, reflex-conditioned behavior of the lower forms of animal life." *American Journal of Public Health*, vol. 45, November, 1955, p. 1480.
2. Hawley, Paul R., "Evaluation of the Quality of Patient Care," *American Journal of Public Health*, vol. 45, December, 1955, p. 1533.
3. The literature is replete with critical comment concerning the current

state of evaluative research. See, for example, Roscoe Kandle's plea that "a fresh start be made in the evaluation of public health practices, with renewed ambition and new perspectives." Report of First National Conference on Evaluation in Public Health, "Evaluation in Public Health," *Public Health Reports,* vol. 71, June, 1956, p. 527.

4. For example, summaries of such reports and discussions for the field of public health may be found in Herzog, Elizabeth, *Some Guide Lines for Evaluative Research,* U.S. Department of Health, Education, and Welfare, Social Security Administration, Children's Bureau, Washington, 1959; *Evaluation in Mental Health,* U.S. Department of Health, Education, and Welfare, Public Health Service, Publication No. 413, Government Printing Office, Washington, 1955; Price, Bronson, *School Health Services: A Selective Review of Evaluative Studies,* U.S. Department of Health, Education, and Welfare, Social Security Administration, Children's Bureau, Washington, 1957; *First National Conference on Evaluation in Public Health,* School of Public Health, University of Michigan, Continued Education Series No. 89, Ann Arbor, 1960; Getting, Vlado A., "The Medical Officer's Bookshelf on Epidemiology and Evaluation: Part II, Evaluation," *American Journal of Public Health,* vol. 47, April, 1957, pp. 408–413; *Planning Evaluations of Mental Health Programs,* Milbank Memorial Fund, New York, 1958; Gruenberg, Ernest M., editor. *Evaluating the Effectiveness of Mental Health Services,* Milbank Memorial Fund Quarterly, vol. 44, part 2, January, 1966. (Entire issue.)

5. "A Critique of Community Public Health Services," *American Journal of Public Health,* vol. 47, November, 1957, p. 38.

6. The growth of statistical indices for evaluative purposes is presented in more detail in Ciocco, Antonio, "On Indices for the Appraisal of Health Department Activities," *Journal of Chronic Diseases,* vol. 11, May, 1960, pp. 509–522.

7. Early efforts of the American Public Health Association in this regard are described in Hiscock, Ira V., "Surveying Community Needs," *American Journal of Public Health,* vol. 41, part 2, January, 1951, pp. 37–50.

8. Emerson, Haven, "Public Health Diagnosis," *Journal of Preventive Medicine,* vol. 1, 1927, p. 401.

9. Chapin offers an interesting description of the public health movement and the growth of concern with evaluation. See Chapin, Charles V., "History of State and Municipal Control of Disease," in *A Half Century of Public Health,* American Public Health Association, New York, 1921, p. 133–160.

10. *Appraisal Form for City Health Work,* 1925, 1926, 1929, 1934; *Evaluation Schedule for Use in the Study and Appraisal of Community Health Programs,* 1943, 1947; *Guide to a Community Health Study,* 1955, 1961, Committee on Administrative Practice, American Public Health Association, New York. It is revealing to note the kinds of questions that are asked in these Evaluation Schedules: "Is a typhoid carrier registry kept? By whom? Number of carriers now under supervision. Restrictions on car-

riers. Number of diagnostic observations in regard to venereal disease performed during year. Cases reported and contacts reported, followed up, and examined. Do laboratories report positive findings to the local health department? Total births delivered by physicians, midwives. Are all maternal deaths in the health jurisdiction reviewed? By whom? Number of prematures at home visited by public health nurses within 18 hours of reporting."

11. A brief history of these efforts at evaluation is given in Palmer, George T., "The Evaluation of Community Health Programs," in Emerson, Haven, editor, *Administrative Medicine,* Williams and Wilkins Co., Baltimore, 1919, pp. 923–936.

12. As pointed out by Vlado Getting, "This APHA Evaluation Schedule, although at present outdated and therefore little used, has served as a model for the development of many reports, appraisals, or evaluation reports required from local health departments by states. . . . The Evaluation Schedule has served well to assist health officers to measure the effectiveness of their programs, to obtain community support, and to back up budgetary requests." Getting, Vlado A., "Evaluation," *op. cit.,* p. 410.

13. Syndenstricker, Edgar, "The Measurement of Results in Public Health Work," *Annual Report of the Milbank Memorial Fund,* New York, 1926, pp. 1–35.

14. See Ciocco, Antonio, *op. cit.,* for an excellent critique of the types of indices used in appraisal forms.

15. In one sense this was not so much a new direction as a return to the original focus of the public service movement upon community social problems affecting the welfare of the public. Historically the field of public service had its origins in the social reform movements of the nineteenth century. See Leavell, Hugh R., "Medical Progress: Contributions of the Social Sciences to the Solution of Health Problems," *New England Journal of Medicine,* vol. 247, December 4, 1952, p. 894.

16. As defined by the World Health Organization, "Health is a state of complete physical, mental and social well-being and not merely the absence of disease or infirmity." *Constitution of the World Health Organization of the United Nations,* World Health Organization, Geneva, Switzerland, 1946.

17. For a discussion of social forces in public health today, see Suchman, Edward A., *Sociology and the Field of Public Health,* Russell Sage Foundation, New York, 1963; also Wolff, George, "Social Pathology as a Medical Science," *American Journal of Public Health,* vol. 42, December, 1952, pp. 1576–1582.

18. Knutson, Andie L., "Evaluating Program Progress," *Public Health Reports,* vol. 70, March, 1955, pp. 305–310.

19. "The illustrations make it clear that a community agency sincerely interested in measuring the effects of its activities on the health of the people *must be willing to establish a research program for this purpose,*" Ciocco, Antonio, *op. cit.,* p. 521.

20. Fleck, Andrew C., Jr., "Evaluation as a Logical Process," *Canadian Journal of Public Health*, vol. 52, May, 1961, pp. 185–191.
21. Greenberg, Bernard G., and Berwyn F. Mattison, "The Whys and Wherefores of Program Evaluation," *Canadian Journal of Public Health*, vol. 46, July, 1955, pp. 293–299.
22. In discussing evaluation in a large city health department, Baumgartner has this to say: "I cannot cite one important instance when a director of a large ongoing program has submitted a plan for evaluation to determine whether the program should or should not be continued. . . . It is a rare administrator who can put years of effort into any activity and then seriously consider whether his work has been valuable or useless." Baumgartner, Leona, "Research—A Keystone of Development in Public Health Practice." Report presented at Annual Meeting of Pennsylvania Public Health Association, University Park, Pa., August 18, 1959.
23. James, George, "Research by Local Health Depatrtments—Problems, Methods, Results," *American Journal of Public Health*, vol. 48, March, 1958, p. 354.
24. *Evaluation in Mental Health, op. cit.*, p. 1.
25. This point is well demonstrated in MacMahon, Brian, Thomas F. Pugh, and George B. Hutchison, "Principles in the Evaluation of Community Mental Health Programs," *American Journal of Public Health*, vol. 51, July, 1961, pp. 963–968.

CHAPTER III

Concepts and Principles of Evaluation

Currently, the term "evaluation," despite its widespread popularity, is poorly defined and often improperly used. For the most part, its meaning is taken for granted and very few attempts have been made, even by those most concerned, to formulate any conceptually rigorous definition or to analyze the main principles of its use. The result is wide disagreement, with many other terms such as "assessment," "appraisal," and "judgment" often being used interchangeably with evaluation.

More serious than this looseness of definition is the absence of any clear-cut understanding of the basic requirements of evaluative research. One finds a wide variety of statistical records, inventories, surveys, testimonials, and experiments all classified as evaluation studies. Such studies vary from the "Is everyone happy?" approach to complex experimental designs. They include highly subjective assessments and detailed statistical analyses. As a consequence, the field of evaluative research is notable for its lack of comparability and cumulativeness of findings. Different results obtained for different purposes by different methods and based on different criteria lead to a confusion which is doubly difficult to resolve in the frequent absence of any explicit statement of objectives or methods of procedure by the evaluator.

The purpose of this chapter is to examine the various uses of the term "evaluation" and the different ways in which evaluation studies are conducted in an attempt to make evaluative research more systematic. While it would be premature and pretentious to offer a framework upon which all might be expected to agree, we do believe that an analysis of the key dimensions of the evaluation process will help greatly to further common understanding and to advance the field of evaluative research. First, we propose to examine various definitions of evaluation, both conceptual and operational; second, to relate evaluative research to two main elements in evaluation—values and objectives; and third, to discuss various types and classifications of evaluative research. This conceptual analysis, we hope, will constitute a first step toward the future development of a "theory and method" of evaluation.

CONCEPTS OF EVALUATION

An examination of the use of the term "evaluation" in the literature reveals an inextricable mixture of conceptual and operational definitions—with the greater emphasis being upon the latter. The conceptual definitions, for the most part, do not attempt any logical formality but rather offer a list of characteristics descriptive of evaluation as a cognitive and affective process. The operational definitions concentrate upon the purposes of evaluation and the procedures involved in conducting an evaluation study. This is not especially surprising in an area lacking any formalization of theory or method and is probably a necessary precursor to the development of a more systematic approach.

To begin with, the American Public Health Association offers the following conceptual *and* operational definition in its "Glossary of Administrative Terms in Public Health."[1]

> The process of determining the value or amount of success in achieving a predetermined objective. It includes at least the following steps: Formulation of the objective, identification of the proper criteria to be used in measuring success, determination and explanation of the degree of success, recommendations for further program activity.

The key conceptual elements in this definition are "the value or amount of success" and "predetermined objective," while the significant operational terms are "objective," "criteria," and "determination and explanation of the degree of success." Thus, inherent in evaluation is the process of assigning value to some objective and then determining the degree of success in attaining this valued objective. These two ideas are recognized quite explicitly by Riecken, who defines evaluation as "the measurement of desirable and undesirable consequences of an action that has been taken in order to forward some goal that we value."[2]

Riecken introduces two further concepts in his definition: (1) the object of study in evaluation is some activity; and (2) this activity may have negative as well as the desired positive consequences. In this sense an evaluation study presupposes the existence of some program or activity to be evaluated. Thus, we now locate evaluation in the area of programmatic or goal-oriented activity and recognize that the activity will have multiple effects, some of which may be undesirable. Riecken further delimits the evaluation process when he concludes that any intentional social action can be the object of an evaluation study. According to this approach, the activity being evaluated will usually be one of deliberate social change; in other words, evaluation is the process whereby man attempts to check upon his own ability to influence other men or his environment. This definition of evaluation is supported by Borgatta, who finds that "research problems in evaluative research . . . recur in the many circumstances where programs operate manifestly to improve existing conditions, or where efforts are being made to prevent or stop deterioration of existing conditions."[3]

This emphasis upon social change as the subject of evaluation study is underscored by Hyman, who defines evaluation as "the procedures of fact-finding about the results of planned social action."[4] Hyman's definition clearly identifies evaluation as a form of "applied" research whose major objective is not the production of new basic knowledge but rather the study of the effectiveness of the application of such knowledge. This distinction between evaluative and basic research is also stressed by the Subcommittee on Evaluation of Mental Health Activities of the National Advisory Mental Health Council as follows: "Evaluation thus connotes scientific method, but has characteristics that distinguish it from that type of research whose objective is the accumulation and analysis of data in order to formulate hypotheses and theory for the sake of new knowledge itself, irrespective of judgment of the value of the knowledge."[5]

"Effectiveness" is the key term in the definition offered by several other research workers. Greenberg and Mattison would restrict evaluation to the "follow-up" of results. "Evaluation of public health programs should denote a measurement of the effectiveness of the program. This effectiveness should be measured in terms of the fulfillment of the program's objectives."[6] James states simply, "Program evaluation can be defined as the measurement of success in reaching a stated objective,"[7] while Anderson qualifies the reaching of the objective in terms of "measuring achievement of *progress* toward predetermined goals."[8] Anderson would go farther in his definition of goals by examining the value of the goals themselves. "It is also concerned with determining whether the goals themselves are valid."[9] As we shall see later, the relationship of objectives to their underlying assumptions is, indeed, a crucial aspect of evaluative research.

While very few discussions of evaluation in the literature attempt to formulate conceptual definitions, almost all do offer some operational definitions in terms of either what evaluation tries to do or how it proceeds. According to this approach, one recognizes a study as being evaluative by its purpose or its method. In general, whenever one asks such questions as—"How good is the program?" "What effects are we having?" "Is the program working as we expected?"—and uses such instruments as rating sheets, appraisal forms, evaluation guides, or research designs which involve comparing accomplishment before or after or in the presence or absence of a particular action, one may be said to be conducting an evaluation study. Thus, Klineberg defines evaluation as "a process which enables the administrator to describe the effects of his programme, and thereby to make progressive adjustments in order to reach his goals more effectively."[10] Bigman expands upon these purposes of evaluation by listing six main uses of an evaluation study:[11]

1. To discover whether and how well objectives are being fulfilled.
2. To determine the reasons for specific successes and failures.
3. To uncover the principles underlying a successful program.
4. To direct the course of experiments with techniques for increasing effectiveness.
5. To lay the basis for further research on the reasons for the relative success of alternative techniques.
6. To redefine the means to be used for attaining objectives, and even to redefine subgoals, in the light of research findings.

These purposes strongly suggest an almost intrinsic relationship between evaluation and program planning and development. Evaluative research provides the basic information for designing and redesigning action programs. Just as nonevaluative research holds out the hope of increased understanding of basic processes, so does evaluative research aim at an increased understanding of applied or administrative processes. Thus, according to Klineberg's definition, the goal of evaluative research extends beyond simply determining success or failure toward knowing why success or failure occurred and what can be done about it. Evaluation, in this sense, involves more than judging; it also encompasses understanding and redefinition.

This emphasis of evaluation upon the analysis, as well as the measurement of effectiveness, is implied in some of the questions proposed by Herzog for "a satisfactory evaluation of effort":[12]

1. What kind of change is desired?
2. By what means is change to be brought about?
3. What is the evidence that the changes observed are due to the means employed?
4. What is the meaning of the changes found?
5. Were there unexpected consequences?

These questions also point up the kinds of methodological problems that are likely to arise in the course of making an evaluation study. These methodological problems are the focus of attention of a comprehensive review of evaluation research in the field of mental health. The major concern is with the reliability and validity of the measures of effectiveness and with an understanding of the reasons for success or failure. This review lists the following six steps as essential for evaluation:

1. Identification of the goals to be evaluated.
2. Analysis of the problems with which the activity must cope.
3. Description and standardization of the activity.
4. Measurement of the degree of change that takes place.
5. Determination of whether the observed change is due to the activity or to some other cause.
6. Some indication of the durability of the effects.[13]

These conditions for evaluative research clearly place evaluation within the camp of scientific research and will be discussed in detail in the following chapters on methodology. But what, then, do we do with the overwhelming majority of hundreds of evaluation studies that do not and cannot satisfy these standards of scientific methodology? This is a major question for the field of evaluation today in such public service fields as health, education, and social welfare. Certainly, as Anderson points out, evaluation studies today are made for different purposes, use different methods, have different objectives and criteria for measuring success in attaining these objectives.[14]

Based on this awareness that an evaluation study may take several different forms and a recognition that the primary function of most evaluation studies is to aid in the planning, development, and operation of service programs, we would like to propose a distinction between *evaluation* as the general process of judging the worthwhileness of some activity regardless of the method employed, and *evaluative research* as the specific use of the scientific method for the purpose of making an evaluation. This separation of evaluation as a goal from evaluative research as a particular means of attaining that goal would then permit one to classify evaluation studies according to different objectives or purposes and according to the type of method used. Examples of these different bases for classifying evaluation studies will be given in a later section.

For the present, we may simply indicate the range of variation by defining evaluation as the determination (whether based on opinions, records, subjective or objective data) of the results (whether desirable or undesirable; transient or permanent; immediate or delayed) attained by some activity (whether a program, or part of a program, a drug or a therapy, an ongoing or one-shot approach) designed to accomplish some valued goal or objective (whether ultimate, intermediate, or immediate, effort or performance, long or short range). This definition contains four key dimensions: (1) process—the "determination"; (2) criteria—the "results"; (3) stimulus—the "activity"; and (4) value—the "objective." The scientific method with its accompanying research techniques then provides the most promising means for "determining" the relationship of the "stimulus" to the "objective" in terms of measurable "criteria."

This does not rule out the use of "nonscientific" methods for evaluation, even if it clearly places a premium upon the use of "scientific" methodology. The emphasis, however, is where it belongs—upon the evaluation process as a goal rather than upon evaluative research as one means toward attaining that goal. There are many evaluational questions in program planning, development, and operation which can be answered without research, and many, in our present state of knowledge, that cannot be answered even if the best research techniques are used. Evaluative research is a tool, and like all tools, to be most effective, it must be designed for a specific function. The one final caution we would like to add is that the evaluator must be aware of which tool he is using and, if the evaluation requires a scientific research approach, that he does not substitute a subjective appraisal. It is also our conviction that the need today is for more scientific evaluative research and that greater progress in evaluation will be made the more one attempts to examine the objectives of a particular program including the underlying assumptions, develops measurable criteria specifically related to these objectives, and then sets up a controlled situation to determine the extent to which these objectives, and any negative side effects, are achieved. The satisfaction of these three basic requirements is the *sine qua non* of evaluative research that is truly research and not just subjective judgment.

EVALUATION AND VALUES

One of the major concepts appearing constantly throughout the above discussion is that of *values*. The value-laden nature of one's objectives constitutes a major distinction between evaluative research and basic research aimed at hypothesis-testing. A precondition to an evaluation study is the presence of some activity whose objectives are assumed to have value. In this section, we will attempt to make a little more explicit this relationship between values and the evaluation process.

"Value" may be defined as any aspect of a situation, event, or object that is invested with a preferential interest as being "good," "bad," "desirable," "undesirable," or the like. As defined by King, "values are the principles by which we establish priorities and hierarchies of importance among needs, demands, and goals."[15] Clearly, value orientations are highly relevant to all public services and to other areas of purposeful human activity. Such values, on the part of both professionals and the public, do much to determine the objectives of public service programs, the kinds of program operations that may be established, and the degree of success achieved by these programs.

Values are modes of organizing human activity—meaningful, affectively charged principles which determine both the goals of public service and social action programs and the acceptable means of attaining these goals. Such values may be *inherent* in the object or activity itself, or they may be *conceived* as being present whether they really are or are not. They may be *operative* as determinants of behavior, or they may have little actual influence on behavior. The relationships between inherent, conceived, and operative values vary greatly from area to area and are largely a matter for empirical investigation.[16] These relationships are obviously of tremendous importance in analyzing the objectives and underlying assumptions of any public service program. For example, any program designed to reduce the incidence of lung cancer by changing the smoking habits of individuals must first establish the *inherent* value of smoking as a cause of lung cancer, then it must create within smokers the *conceived* value of the undesirability of dying from lung cancer, which finally must be translated into the *operative* value of giving up cigarettes as a preferred form of enjoyment. As we shall see later, public service values at times may not coincide with people's values.

It may be helpful to visualize the evaluation process as a circular one, stemming from and returning to the formation of values, as shown in Figure 1.

Evaluation always starts with some value, either explicit or implicit—for example, it is good to live a long time; then a goal is formulated derived from this value. The selection of goals is usually preceded by or concurrent with *"value formation."* An example of *"goal-setting"* would be the statement that fewer people should develop coronary disease, or that not so many people should die from cancer. Goal-setting forces are always in competition with each other for money, resources, and effort.

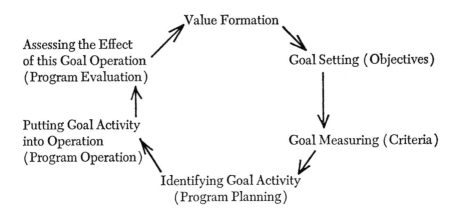

Figure 1. EVALUATION PROCESS

There next has to be some way of *"measuring goal attainment."* If we set as our goal that fewer people should die from cancer, then we need some means of discovering how many are presently dying from cancer (for example, vital statistics). The nature of the evaluation will depend largely on the type of measure we have available to determine the attainment of our objective.

The next step in the process is the identification of some kind of *"goal-attaining activity."* In the case of cancer, for example, a program of cancer-detecting activities aimed at early detection and treatment might be considered. Then the goal-attaining activity is put into operation. Diagnostic centers are set up and people urged to come in for check-ups.

Then, at some point, we have the *assessment* of this goal-directed operation. This stage includes the evaluation of the degree to which the operating program has achieved the predetermined objectives. As stated previously, this assessment may be scientifically done or it may not.

Finally, on the basis of the assessment, a *judgment* is made as to whether the goal-directed activity was worthwhile. This brings us back to value formation. Someone now may say that it is "good" to have cancer diagnostic centers. At the end of the evaluation process, we may get a new value, or we may reaffirm, reasses, or redefine an old value. For example, if the old value was "It is good to live a long time," the new value might be, "It is good to live until 100 if you remain healthy, but if you can't remain healthy it's better not to live past eighty."

In actuality, when the evaluation process begins, activities may be, and usually are, already going on.[18] The evaluator may come in at any point.

Starting with one's basic values may appear logical, but in reality there is an ongoing matrix of activity which the evaluator must dissect into its components. It is not necessary to begin at the value formation stage. Values may already be formed and goals already set. Nor is the sequence of operations in the process invariable. Almost any combination of simultaneous operations is possible.

Let us examine another illustration of the evaluation process. Suppose we begin with the value that it is better for people to have their own teeth rather than false teeth. We may then set as our goal that people shall retain their teeth as long as possible. As a measure of our goal, we might count how many people have lost their teeth and at what ages. In effect, identifying a measure of our goal usually determines the indicators we will use of having attained that goal. Then we plan a goal-directed activity. In this case, we might decide to put dentists into the public schools to detect dental problems early, on the assumption that this will reduce the loss of teeth in later life. Now we put our goal activity into operation—we obtain the services of the dentists and set up the school clinics. Next we want to find out the effect of our goal-activity operation—is it, indeed, saving teeth that would otherwise be lost? There are many ways of doing this from the elaborate scientific model involving control groups and rigorous experimental conditions to the least scientific use of self-designated experts testifying that the program is working well. Finally, we return to value formation. In this example, an administrator may say the dental program is working so well in one place it ought to be introduced into other places as well.

The foregoing description of the evaluation process strongly underscores the close interrelationship between evaluation and program planning and operation, and touches upon the possibility of a conflict in values between the program administrator and the evaluator. These problems will be discussed in more detail in the chapter dealing with the administrative considerations in program evaluation.

Implicit in any action program intended to change the knowledge, attitudes, or behavior of the public are the values of the professional group desiring to produce this change. The definition of evaluation as the study of the effectiveness of planned social change would indicate the highly value-laden context of evaluative research. Even on a very general level, a value premise exists that change is good, that it can be planned and brought about. Underlying such a value premise one can often find other presumptions, such as if people are rational and properly instructed and informed, they can be relied upon to do the "right" thing. Perhaps the most common assumption here is that information can lead to a change in one's attitude and that changed attitudes will result in changed behavior.[19] Another common assumption is that any action is better than doing nothing, and that effort, in and of itself, is a sign of accomplishment.[20]

This problem of values and social change has been treated extensively by social scientists and need not concern us beyond pointing out the intimate relationship between values, social change, and evaluation.[21, 22] As analyzed by Foster in relation to intercultural health programs, "directed culture change" refers to the recognition of and conscious attempt to meet social problems. Such directed change usually involves an interference with the community's customary way of life and needs to take other values besides those of the innovator into account. "Intercultural health programs require decisions and action which some people will feel violate their rights."[23]

Public service in general, as a professional form of activity dedicated to social planning and change, is naturally highly permeated by value judgments. Both the goals or objectives of public service and the means to be used in attaining these objectives are subject to professional and public determinations of what is "acceptable and appropriate." A keen awareness of these professional and public forces, and of the conflicts that are inevitable both within the professional and public groups and between the profession and the public is essential for any intelligent evaluation of the success or failure of a public service program. Social values in large part set the boundaries of a social problem and determine the nature of any remedial actions.

We cannot in this report discuss the basic value orientations of the various fields of public service or analyze the major sources of internal and external conflict. This is an important area which has not received the attention it warrants from those concerned with public service planning and evaluation.[24] Occasionally, when the conflict becomes unavoidable, as in the case of medical care for the aged, the battle lines are more clearly drawn and the underlying assumptions of what is or is not a public service responsibility come to the fore. Areas of conflict are bound to increase as the distinction between preventive, treatment, and rehabilitative programs becomes increasingly difficult to maintain. Certainly, for example, the World Health Organization's definition of health as "a state of complete physical, mental, and social well-being and not merely the absence of disease or infirmity,"[25] while admittedly more a statement of creed than a blueprint for services, sounds a call for a much broader interpretation of what should be considered successful public health action.

From the point of view of evaluation, conflicting values introduce serious problems for the determination of the criteria by which the success of a public service program is to be judged. As Parsons has indicated, medicine constitutes only one subsystem in American society which may have values and goals in conflict with other subsystems.[26] For example, population control is a crucial area of public health and welfare concern, but the values and goals of our religious subsystem strongly influence the nature and success of programs involving the use of contraceptive measures. The economic subsystem is constantly pointing to both the economic costs and consequences of public service activities as a major criterion to be taken into consideration in evaluating service programs.[27] Political forces combine with economic forces in support of or opposition to any form of "socialized" medicine.[28] Thus, a public service program may be judged desirable or successful according to one scheme of values and undesirable or unsuccessful according to another.

Sigerest has stressed the dependence of medicine and public health upon the social, economic, and political structure of a society.[29] Such current public health problems as air pollution, fluoridation, narcotics addiction, venereal disease, accident prevention, radiation, use of insecticides, and smoking, to name a few, will have to be met within the arena of public controversy over means and ends.[30] Both the extent to which public health should attempt to institute programs in these areas and the type of program to be established are subjects of heated debate. As stated by a public health professional, "Having only recently emerged scarred and nonvictorious from the battlefield of cigarette smoking versus cancer of the lung, I can testify that the dairy and beef trusts, as well as the hamburger and custard stands, will not willingly give up their vested and powerful interests."[31]

There can be little question that values play a large role in determining the objectives of public service programs and that any evaluation study of the desirable and undesirable consequences of such programs must take social values, especially conflicting values, into account. In the next section, we will look more specifically at the way in which values and assumptions affect the formulation of objectives for evaluative research.

OBJECTIVES AND ASSUMPTIONS

The most identifying feature of evaluative research is the presence of some goal or objective whose measure of attainment constitutes the main focus of the research problem. Evaluation cannot exist in a vacuum. One must always ask evaluation "of what." Every action, every program has some value for some purpose—therefore, it is meaningless to ask whether a program has any value without specifying value for what. Gruenberg makes this point quite emphatically when he argues, "I feel strongly that evaluation research requires of the investigators that they force the administrative structure they are investigating to specify the values that the administration is seeking, at least to the point where some visible research question is specified. And if there is no *value* being sought by a service, I don't see how you would do evaluation work."[32] In reverse, if any activity has an objective, then it can be made the subject of evaluative research. Thus, one may evaluate not only action programs, but one may also evaluate a research project in terms of the degree to which it successfully attains it own objectives, that is, the test of some hypothesis, or even a research technique in terms of its ability to produce reliable, valid, and relevant data bearing on an hypothesis.[33]

Given the basic importance of a clear statement of the program objectives to be evaluated, it is not difficult to understand why so many evaluation studies which fail to define these objectives prove unproductive. This is tantamount to undertaking a basic research project without first formulating one's hypotheses. An evaluation project may be viewed as a study of change—the program to be evaluated constitutes the stimulus or "causal" or independent variable, while the desired change is similar to the "effect" or dependent variable. Characterized this way, one may formulate an evaluation project in terms of a series of hypotheses which state that "Activities A, B, and C will produce results X, Y, and Z." Note that this formulation requires both a statement of the end result, or objectives of the program, *and* the specification of what it is about the program that might be expected to produce these results. In the chapters on methodology we will carry this analogy farther when we discuss the problem of establishing causal connections between one's activities and one's results.

The clear-cut definition of program objectives and the identification of the responsible program activities is not an easy task. As Hyman so clearly points out, "The many difficulties suggested—the breadth of the thing subsumed under a particular objective, the multiple objectives encompassed by many programs, the ambiguity inherent in any or all of the objectives as stated, and the disagreement as to the objectives—are characteristic of many programs and are enough to stagger the imagination of the evaluator."[34]

Some of the difficult questions that arise involve the *kind* of change desired, the *means* by which this change is to be brought about, and the *signs* by which such change is to be recognized.[35] In regard to the definition of the kind of change, one must be able to specify change from what to what. One must be able to determine the existing state of affairs before the program activity is initiated and then to define what the desired change is to be. Thus, before one can evaluate the success of an action program, one must be able to diagnose the presence or absence of a social problem and to define goals indicative of progress in ameliorating that condition.[36] Greenberg and Mattison draw a direct parallel between the clinical process aimed at diagnosing what is wrong and prescribing a course of treatment which can then be evaluated in terms of the patient's progress and the public health process of determining community health needs, developing public health programs to meet these needs, and following up these programs to evaluate their success or failure.[37]

The specific procedures for formulating significant program objectives, for deciding upon the criteria by which the achievement of these goals will be judged, and for developing reliable and valid measures of these criteria constitute basic methodological problems in evaluative research and will be discussed in the following chapters on research design. At the present time we wish only to raise some of the more general considerations involved in the formulation of objectives for evaluative research. Among the more compelling of these are the following:

1. *What* is the nature of the content of the objective? Are we interested in changing knowledge, attitudes, and/or behavior? Are we concerned with producing exposure, awareness, interest, and/or action? Answers to these questions permit the evaluator to determine what Hyman calls the "regions within which the concepts are set."[38] Hovland and his colleagues in evaluating the effectiveness of propaganda films, for example, specify four different areas of interest: knowledge, beliefs, attitudes, and motivations.[39] As we shall see later, public service programs may operate on different levels of objective, ranging from the ultimate one of preventing a problem from developing to the more immediate one of distributing information on the problem.

2. *Who* is the target of the program? At which groups in the population is the program aimed? Are we seeking to change individuals, groups, or whole communities?[40] Are we seeking to reach the target group directly or indirectly through some related target group such as friends or relatives?[41] These questions help to identify the present and potential "clients" for a public service program and serve to define the population to

be studied. In general, we may distinguish between programs aimed at the large-scale, undifferentiated mass or public-as-a-whole; at discrete target groups viewed as the direct objects of change; or at indirect groups conceived as sources of influence upon the ultimate target group. Any program will have differential effects among various segments of the population and success or failure can only be measured in terms of whom one is attempting to reach. The evaluation literature is full of examples of self-selected audiences already favorably disposed or involved, thus constituting highly biased groups for evaluative purposes.[42]

3. *When* is the desired change to take place? Are we seeking an immediate effect or are we gradually building toward some postponed effect? In general, we may talk about short-term, discrete programs of a single, one-shot nature; cyclical or repetitive programs that are continuously renewed; or long-term, developmental programs that keep building toward some long-range goal. Some objectives take longer than others to attain and the evaluation must take into account the length of time that the program has been in effect.[43] Many evaluation studies show immediate signs of success only to have these disappear as the novelty and enthusiasm of a new program wear off.[44] Other programs appear to be unsuccessful at first, but create a type of "sleeper" effect which shows up at a later time. Related to this question is one on how long one expects or desires the effect to last. Not all programs aim at the same degree of permanent or transient change.[45]

4. Are the objectives *unitary or multiple?* Is the program aimed at a single change or at a series of changes? Are these changes the same for all people or do they vary for different groups of people? It is rare that any program will have only one purpose or one effect. This means that the evaluator must usually provide for the measurement of multiple effects requiring the allocation of priorities for study. It also means careful attention to unanticipated or undesirable "side effects."[46] As in the case of evaluating the effects of drugs, one must always be on the alert for contraindications.

5. What is the desired *magnitude* of effect? Are we seeking widespread or concentrated results? Do we have to attain any particular proportion of effectiveness before the program can be considered a success? Are there any specified standards of accomplishment that we have to meet? Too many programs assume unrealistic goals of total success. The objectives for most action programs must be much more modest, involving amelioration rather than elimination and aimed at lessened damage and better functioning rather than total prevention.[47]

6. *How* is the objective to be attained? What means are to be used to put the program across? Will one depend primarily on voluntary cooperation or will an attempt be made to secure legal sanctions? Will personal or impersonal, formal or informal appeals be made? To an increasing extent public service programs will have to relinquish their dependence upon legislative action and seek community support for their objectives. This will greatly increase the need for social action programs to find ways and means which appeal to the public and which do not require a high degree of motivation or personal inconvenience.

These six considerations deal with basic questions that need to be answered in formulating the objectives of a program for the sake of evaluation.[48] While some of these questions may be irrelevant for operational purposes, they play a crucial role in determining which objectives one selects for evaluation and how one designs the evaluation study. Such methodological problems as sampling, selection of controls, preparation of measuring instruments, method of field administration, and techniques of analysis are strongly affected by the kinds of answers one gives to the questions specified above, as will be shown in the chapters on methodology. It is also probable that, in the course of seeking answers to these questions in an evaluation study, the program administrator will find himself forced to sharpen his own picture of what he is attempting to do.

Many of the answers to the questions raised above will require an examination of the underlying assumptions of the stated objectives. This is to be expected, since inherent in the idea of evaluation is a critical attitude of mind, a challenging of the status quo. An evaluation rarely takes place in an atmosphere of complacency and satisfaction. The call to evaluate is usually the result of dissatisfaction somewhere. Where everyone takes it for granted that a program is successful, there will be little pressure for evaluation.

The process of seeking to understand the underlying assumptions of an objective is akin to that of questioning the validity of one's hypothesis. Involved is a concern with the theoretical basis of one's belief that "activity A will produce effect B." Such concerns are the earmark of professional growth. So long as one proceeds on faith in accepted procedures without questioning the basis for this faith, one is functioning as a technician rather than a professional. The future development of the various fields of public service as science as well as art will depend to a large extent upon their willingness to challenge the underlying assumptions of their program objectives. As stated by James and Hilleboe, "It [evaluation] is after all primarily a critical point of view. It becomes a question of proving to scientific colleagues how we know our efforts have been successful, what assumptions were required in order to establish this proof, and what degree of confidence we demand for these assumptions."[49]

Assumptions may be classified into two types—value assumptions and validity assumptions. Value assumptions pertain to the system of beliefs concerning what is "good" within a society or a subgroup of that society. Thus, we may have such almost universally accepted value assumptions as, "Human life is worth saving"; "Unnecessary suffering is bad"; "Good health is to be desired." One might say that the main objectives of the public service movement itself are based upon the value assumption that the government owes its people protection from undesirable social conditions. Such value assumptions, as we have noted previously, may vary from group to group and result in value conflicts that create public controversy over goals and means of public service programs. These conflicts are implied in the evaluative question, "Success from whose point of view?"

Validity assumptions are much more specifically related to program objectives. Such assumptions, for example, underlie our belief that the cause for much perinatal mortality may be found in a lack of care during pregnancy and that prenatal clinics which supply information to expectant mothers can improve such care and result in a reduction in perinatal mortality. These validity assumptions help to explain the current move from mental institutions to home care based on the belief that people are better off at home than in institutions. A basic validity assumption underlying mass chronic disease detection programs is that those people who are found to have a chronic disease are "better off" than they would have been had the disease not been detected.[50] Similar validity assumptions lie behind the recommendation to see one's physician regularly for preventive check-ups. The Subcommittee on Evaluation of Mental Health Activities lists the following validity assumptions as the basic rationale for many mental health programs:[51]

> Community clinics will save many patients from State hospitals.
> The basis of prevention is correction of faulty child-rearing practices and the treatment of emotional disorders in childhood.
> Mental health is a state for which individuals can be educated by disseminating knowledge about emotional processes through pamphlets, popular books, movies, posters, exhibits, radio, television, and lectures.
> Unconscious psychological determinants are the major explanation of maladaptive reactions.

One has only to look at random through the 1960 *Guide to a Community Health Study* for similar statements of assumptions whose validity is taken for granted as the basis for setting up public health programs. For example, in regard to *housing*—"Healthful housing is paramount to the attainment of a healthful life" (page 166); in regard to obesity—"Weight control programs in the community provide opportunities through group or individual discussion for persons to reach and maintain optimum weight" (page 104); in regard to schools—"The environmental conditions of lighting, heating, ventilation, etc., have a direct bearing on the efficiency of learning, and play an important part in forming attitudes of the future community leaders towards cleanliness" (page 168).[52]

Obviously, all programs designed to produce change must make validity assumptions concerning the worthwhileness of their services. It is impossible to secure proof of the effectiveness of everything one wishes to do. Nor is it desirable. Operating personnel must proceed on the basis of the best available knowledge at the time. The question is one of how freely such validity assumptions are made and how much is at stake. Certainly an attempt should be made to identify clearly and objectively as many of the validity assumptions underlying a program as possible—and the more important and consequential the program, the more need there will be to challenge these assumptions. A projected major hospital construction program for the treatment of narcotic addicts, for example, requires much more careful analysis of the assumption that institutionalized treatment is necessary for narcotics addiction[53] than does a community day care center for handicapped children.

The administrator who seeks positive answers to all validity questions before initiating public service programs will spend a great deal of his time and resources in contemplation and offer very few services. He must call upon his own knowledge and skill to develop practical programs whose assumptions are clearly set down. If evaluation is built into the program, then the results may prove or disprove the significance of these assumptions. Should other investigators provide new evidence, he can adjust his objectives accordingly. Hence, when a social science study of health education techniques indicated that these were not effective in motivating people to have tuberculosis x-rays, a health department was able to curtail sharply the further dissipation of its resources in that direction.[54] On the other hand, when several programs on the use of fluoridation for the prevention of dental caries proved the safety and effectiveness of this procedure, health officers throughout the world could urge the addition of up to one part per million of fluoride to a communal water supply in the knowledge that this assumption had now been proved beyond reasonable scientific doubt.[55]

Important elements in the establishment of assumptions are the concepts of validity and reliability. Each assumption assumes the *validity* of an objective, that each objective is a valid means for the achievement of some desired value. This assumption of validity is actually a step toward the refinement of scientific theory. However, while we may assume validity, we are not as free to assume reliability. If we assume a result which actually varies upon repetition by ourselves or other qualified investigators, then we have no fixed point of reference. We may, for example, assume that a screening level of 160 mg. per cent of blood sugar can be used to detect early diabetes, despite the fact that such a screening level will give us a number of false negatives and false positives. Subsequent study will indicate to what degree we are correct and how many false negatives and false positives will appear in our series. However, in making this assumption we must be sure that we are speaking about a particular method of detecting blood glucose; we must be sure that we are performing this procedure on a well-described population, that the tests are run at a given time after a carbohydrate meal and that the blood has been handled in such a way as will not permit the deterioration of the blood sugar in the sample. Unless we have taken these steps to ensure reliability, we will have no certain way of relating our efforts to work done in other areas, to changes which may occur from time to time within our own program, and to future findings in the realm of validity of the test procedure itself. Thus, while we may accept validity on the basis of theory, we must always prove reliability empirically.

The stability of program objectives rests largely upon the reliability of the assumptions made—if we view reliability as the consistency or dependability of these assumptions. Where the underlying assumptions of a program are constantly changing, it is impossible to formulate valid objectives. This is most likely to be the case in problem areas lacking in established theory or factual knowledge. Evaluations of many of the newer programs in public service, such as urban renewal, accident prevention, or population control, suffer from a high degree of inconsistency or disagreement concerning underlying assumptions. It is difficult to compare the relative success of different approaches if these are based on conflicting assumptions. Obviously, programs based on assumptions with low reliability must necessarily have low validity. Since high validity presupposes high reliability, evaluative research usually concerns itself mainly with problems of the validity of the assumptions.

From this discussion of the relationship of evaluation to values, of values to objectives, and of objectives to assumptions, we see that evaluation is inherently a normative subjective process. Borgatta stresses this point when he states: "Professions have norms that may not have a rational basis . . . similarly, with tendencies that are called bureaucratization, institutionalization, and so forth, processes once established tend to be maintained by the authority systems in which they reside. Thus, many things may exist where success or failure of the intended action is not at all clear, yet authority, convention, and other forces may tend to keep them as they are."[56]

This does not mean, however, that one cannot develop objective methods for studying this normative process. It does mean that the form which such evaluative research takes and the criteria of judgment developed need to take into account the importance of existing values to the evaluation process. The following chapter continues this analysis by presenting a classification scheme for evaluation studies based on the relationship of objectives to assumptions and developing categories of evaluative criteria which offer the possibility of more objective research.

NOTES TO CHAPTER III

1. "Glossary of Administrative Terms in Public Health," *American Journal of Public Health*, vol. 50, February, 1960, pp. 225–226.
2. Riecken, Henry W., *The Volunteer Work Camp: A Psychological Evaluation*. Addison-Wesley Press, Cambridge, Mass., 1952, p. 4.
3. Borgatta, Edgar F., "Research Problems in Evaluation of Health Service Demonstrations," *Milbank Memorial Fund Quarterly*, vol. 44, October, 1966, part 2, p. 182.
4. Hyman, Herbert H., Charles R. Wright, and Terence K. Hopkins, *Applications of Methods of Evaluation: Four Studies of the Encampment for Citizenship*. University of California Press, Berkeley, 1962, p. 3.
5. *Evaluation in Mental Health*. U.S. Department of Health, Education, and Welfare, Public Health Service, Publication No. 413, Government Printing Office, Washington, 1955, p. 2.
6. Greenberg, Bernard G., and Berwyn F. Mattison, "The Whys and Wherefores of Program Evaluation," *Canadian Journal of Public Health*, vol. 46, July, 1955, p. 299.

7. James, George, "Planning and Evaluation of Health Programs," in *Administration of Community Health Services*. International City Managers' Association, Chicago, 1961, p. 124.

8. Anderson, Otis L., as reported in *First National Conference on Evaluation in Public Health*, University of Michigan, School of Public Health, Ann Arbor, 1955, p. 7.

9. *Ibid.*, p. 7.

10. Klineberg, Otto, "The Problem of Evaluation," *International Social Science Bulletin*, vol. 7, no. 3, 1955, pp. 346–352.

11. Bigman, Stanley K., "Evaluating the Effectiveness of Religious Programs," *Review of Religious Research*, vol. 2, Winter, 1961, p. 99.

12. Herzog, Elizabeth, *Some Guide Lines for Evaluative Research*, U.S. Department of Health, Education, and Welfare, Social Security Administration, Children's Bureau, Washington, 1959, p. 2.

13. *Evaluation in Mental Health, op. cit.;* see especially p. 21.

14. Anderson, Otis L., *op. cit.*, p. 7.

15. King, Stanley H., *Perceptions of Illness and Medical Practice*. Russell Sage Foundation, New York, 1962, p. 53. In relation to health and disease, King offers the following examples: "The person or group with a time orientation toward the present will have difficulty in seeing the value of inoculations against disease, a future occurrence. Emphasis on collateral relationship to others in distinction to individualistic will cause difficulty in perceiving the importance of taking a person out of a family and putting him in a tuberculosis hospital miles away. The view that man is subjugated to nature may lead an individual not to seek medical help in time of disease, in the belief that the inevitable or fate cannot be overcome. In like vein, this person may not see health as a positive value, much to the dismay of the highly educated physician or public health specialist, who views man as overcoming nature and as able to reach levels of health beyond those of the past." (p. 61)

16. Morris, Charles, *Varieties of Human Value*. University of Chicago Press, Chicago, 1956.

17. This chart was suggested by Jack Elinson.

18. As Vickers states in his analysis of the "goal setting" in public health, "When we open our eyes to the scene around us, we find goals already set. Policies are being implemented, institutions are in action with all the historical momentus of buildings and establishments. Men are in mid-career. Budgets, even budget headings, have acquired prescriptive rights. . . ." Vickers, Geoffrey, "What Sets the Goals of Public Health," *The Lancet*, vol. 1, March, 1958, p. 599.

19. This is the underlying rationale of most health education programs despite increasing evidence of its limited validity. Literally hundreds of evaluation studies in the field of health education have documented the fact that knowledge is rarely a sufficient basis for action. A good review of such studies is given in *Review of Research Related to Health Education Practice*. Health Education Monographs, Supplement No. 1, Society of Public Health Educators, Rye, N.Y., 1963.

20. Williams offers an excellent discussion of the emphasis in American cul-

ture upon rationality and activity as solutions to social problems that is directly applicable to the field of public service. For example, he states, "The Western world generally, however, has tended to unite activity and substantive rationality, focusing upon a choice of the most effective means for a given end. Since systematic wealth-getting, technological achievement, and productive organization of effort have been strongly sanctioned, pressure has been created to search for 'better methods,' with the result that America epitomizes high regard for efficiency in techniques. In this kind of social climate, there is high sensitivity to such epithets as 'backward,' 'inefficient,' 'useless.'" Williams, Robin M., *American Society*, Alfred A. Knopf, Inc., New York, 1952, p. 401.

21. See, for example, Goodenough, Ward H., *Cooperation in Change*, Russell Sage Foundation, New York, 1963.

22. Bennis, Warren G., Kenneth B. Benne, and Robert Chin, editors, *The Planning of Change: Readings in the Applied Behavioral Sciences*. Holt, Rinehart, and Winston, New York, 1961.

23. Foster, George M., *Problems in Intercultural Health Programs*. Social Science Research Council, Pamphlet 12, New York, 1958, pp. 7–8.

24. An exception would be an analysis of social and medical forces influencing public health programs by Sir Geoffrey Vickers. As Vickers points out, "There are, I suggest, three contributions which public health can thus make to the setting of its own goals. It can evaluate health by the criteria which we currently use. It can criticize these criteria and thus help to deepen and refine them. And it can explore those processes of decision by which public health policy is defined and implemented." Vickers, Geoffrey, *op. cit.*, p. 602.

25. *Constitution of the World Health Organization of the United Nations.* World Health Organization, Geneva, Switzerland, 1946.

26. Parsons, Talcott, "Definitions of Health and Illness in the Light of American Values and Social Structure," in Jaco, E. Gartly, editor, *Patients, Physicians, and Illness*. The Free Press, Glencoe, Ill., 1958, pp. 165–187.

27. Economists are particularly concerned with the consequences of public health programs in the underdeveloped areas of the world. By directly affecting the quantity and quality of the labor force, such programs have an important effect on plans for economic development. Myrdal advocates an integrated approach: "An effort to reach permanent improvements of health standards aimed to have a maximum beneficial effect on the well-being of the people will, in other words, have to be integrated in a broad economic and social reform policy." Myrdal, Gunnar, "Economic Aspects of Health," *Chronicle of World Health Organization*, vol. 6, August, 1952, p. 207.

28. Somers, Herman M., and Anne R. Somers, *Doctors, Patients, and Health Insurance*. Doubleday and Co., Garden City, New York, 1962.

29. Roemer, Milton I., editor, *Henry E. Sigerest on the Sociology of Medicine*. M.D. Publications, New York, 1960.

30. Suchman, Edward A., *Sociology and the Field of Public Health*. Russell Sage Foundation, New York, 1963, pp. 58–70.

31. Spain, David M., "Problems in the Study of Coronary Arteriosclerosis in

Population Groups," *Annals of the New York Academy of Sciences*, vol. 84, December 8, 1960, p. 831.

32. Gruenberg, Ernest M., editor, *Evaluating the Effectiveness of Mental Health Services*, Milbank Memorial Fund Quarterly, vol. 44, part 2, January, 1966, p. 353. (Entire issue.)

33. In a very real parallel, the concept of evaluation is similar to that of validity in methodological research. Validity also implies some purpose and, to be meaningful, one must always specify validity for what. Just as early research on validity was held back by a failure to recognize this essential fact, so is evaluative research today greatly confused and subject to needless argument. An insightful discussion of this problem in regard to validity may be found in Stouffer, Samuel A., and others, *Measurement and Prediction*, Princeton University Press, Princeton, N.J., 1949.

34. Hyman, Herbert H., and others, *op. cit.*, p. 7.

35. These questions are raised and discussed in Herzog, Elizabeth, *op. cit.*, pp. 9–36.

36. As several evaluations of mental health programs have pointed out, the difficulty of diagnosing mental illness and of measuring improvement constitute major stumbling blocks in evaluating the success or failure of mental health programs. See, for example, Howe, Louisa P., "Problems in the Evaluation of Mental Health Programs," in Kotinsky, Ruth, and Helen L. Witmer, *Community Programs for Mental Health*, Harvard University Press, Cambridge, Mass., 1955, pp. 225–295.

37. Greenberg, Bernard G., and Berwyn F. Mattison, *op. cit.*, pp. 294–296.

38. Hyman, Herbert H., and others, *op. cit.*, p. 9.

39. Hovland, Carl I., Arthur A. Lumsdaine, and Fred D. Sheffield, *Experiments in Mass Communication*. Princeton University Press, Princeton, N.J., 1949, pp. 33–45.

40. "This population need not be defined as a whole population in the demographic sense, but may be restricted in terms of age, sex, occupation, club or school membership, or in some other way. . . . Depending on the nature of the program to be offered, there may be further specification of the group within the population that is expected to be the particular target of the preventive or therapeutic measures." MacMahon, Brian, Thomas F. Pugh, and George B. Hutchison, "Principles in the Evaluation of Community Mental Health Programs," *American Journal of Public Health*, vol. 51, July, 1961, p. 965.

41. The importance of indirect personal influence in changing behavior has been the subject of a number of public health studies. See, for example, Rosenstock, Irwin, and others, *The Impact of Asian Influenza on Community Life*, U.S. Public Health Service, Publication No. 766, Government Printing Office, Washington, 1960.

42. See, for example, Kline, Nathan S., "Samples and Controls in Psychiatric Research," *Psychiatric Quarterly*, vol. 27, July, 1953, pp. 474–495.

43. Morris, Don P., Eleanor Soroker, and Genette Burruss, "Follow-up Studies of Shy, Withdrawn Children—I. Evaluation of Later Adjustment," *American Journal of Orthopsychiatry*, vol. 24, October, 1954, pp. 743–754.

44. Riecken points out, "All experience with action programs indicates that their real effects cannot be gauged without considering the long-run forces that may support, negate, or even reverse the immediate effects." Riecken, Henry, *op. cit.*, p. 22.

45. Elsewhere, we have developed a classification of public health programs which takes into account both the time dimension and the nature of the target population, as follows (Suchman, Edward A., *op. cit.*, p. 77):

	Target Population	
Time Orientation	Community Support	Individual Behavior
Single action	A	C
Continued action	B	D

46. Opler refers to these as "secondary" and "tertiary" effects. "All plans are sure to have mixed consequences." Opler, Morris E., *Social Aspects of Technical Assistance in Operation.* Tensions and Technology Series, UNESCO, No. 4, Washington, 1954, p. 67.

47. For example, several studies have questioned the value of the current vital statistics system as a yardstick for the measurement of public health needs and accomplishments in chronic disease. See Ciocco, Antonio, "On Indices for the Appraisal of Health Department Activities," *Journal of Chronic Diseases,* vol. 11, May, 1960, pp. 509–522. As stated by Gruenberg, "Death rates, which have ruled the roost for so long as the sole measure of the improvement of a community's health, are insufficient measures of today's public health programs." Gruenberg, Ernest M., "Application of Control Methods to Mental Illness," *American Journal of Public Health,* vol. 47, August, 1957, pp. 944–952.

48. Hutchison lists the three basic questions of evaluative research as: (1) Does the program meet its objectives? (2) To what degree does it meet its objectives? (3) How efficiently are the objectives met? Hutchison, George B., "Evaluation of Preventive Services," *Journal of Chronic Diseases,* vol. 11, May, 1960, pp. 497–508.

49. James, George, and Herman E. Hilleboe, "Evaluation During the Development of a Public Health Program in Chronic Disease," *American Journal of Public Health,* vol. 45, February, 1955, p. 149.

50. Enterline, Philip E., and Bernard Kordan, "A Controlled Evaluation of Mass Surveys for Tuberculosis and Heart Disease," *Public Health Reports,* vol. 73, October, 1958, p. 867.

51. *Evaluation in Mental Health, op. cit.,* pp. 5–6.

52. *Guide to a Community Health Study.* American Public Health Association, New York, 1960.

53. This validity assumption is vigorously challenged in Chein, Isadore, Donald L. Gerard, Robert S. Lee, and Eva Rosenfield, *The Road to H.* Basic Books, New York, 1964. This book marshalls convincing evidence to explode many of the commonly held, preconceived notions about the nature of drug addiction and its treatment.

54. Metzner, Charles A., and Gerald Gurin, *Personal Responses and Social*

Organization in a Health Campaign. University of Michigan, Bureau of Public Health Economics, Research Series No. 9, Ann Arbor, 1960.

55. Arnold, Francis A., Jr., H. Trendley Dean, and John W. Knutson, "Effect of Fluoridated Public Water Supplies on Dental Caries Prevalence," *Public Health Reports,* vol. 68, February, 1953, p. 141.

56. Borgatta, Edgar F., *op. cit.,* p. 183.

CHAPTER IV

Types and Categories of Evaluation

Most programs have multiple objectives. Close examination of these objectives will usually reveal that they consist of a mixture of different dimensions—time, place, method, generality. This multiplicity of objectives is often a source of unproductive disagreement among program personnel and constitutes a major barrier to successful evaluation. As described in a report by a national conference on evaluation, "Where the sections disagreed especially was in the use of time-qualifying adjectives applied to the objectives, such as long-term or short-term objectives. In consulting with these sections, it was obvious that there is a definite lack of uniformity in our terminology. In addition to the above there were long-range, short-range, broad, narrow, subsidiary, subobjective, immediate, intermediate and ultimate objectives."[1]

STATEMENT OF EVALUATIVE OBJECTIVES

A great deal of the confusion regarding objectives could be eliminated by recognizing that these objectives can be classified in a number of different ways, depending upon one's purpose. Perhaps the most common basis for ordering objectives is that of generality. Objectives may range from the most general, that is, a reduction in mortality, to the very specific, that is, reading a health pamphlet. In principle, one may hypothesize an unlimited universe of objectives and subobjectives corresponding to the various steps or actions that make up a total program. While these steps usually comprise a continuous series of events, for evaluation purposes it is essential to subdivide them into some discernible hierarchy of subgoals, each of which may be the result of the successful achievement of the preceding goal and, in turn, a precondition to the next higher goal.

This chain of objectives is often trichotomized in the literature as immediate, intermediate, and ultimate goals. Immediate goals refer to the results of the specific act with which one is momentarily concerned, such as the formation of an obesity club; the intermediate goals push ahead toward the accomplishment of the specific act, such as the actual reduction in weight of club members; the ultimate goal then examines the effect of achieving the intermediate goal upon the health status of the members, such as reduction in the incidence of heart disease.

In a similar vein, Herzog speaks about three types of evaluation studies. "Ultimate evaluation" refers to the determination of the final success of a program in eliminating or reducing the social problem at which it is aimed. "Pre-evaluative research" deals with the intermediate problems that need to be solved before one can attempt ultimate evaluation, such as the development of reliable and valid classifications of the problem, the definition of action goals, and the perfection of tools and techniques. "Short-term evaluation" is limited to seeking specific answers to concrete procedures in terms of immediate utility. Such studies aim only at filling immediate needs concerning the effectiveness of particular acts and attempt to make no generalizations beyond the limits of the data.[2]

The foremost and most all-embracing evaluation deals with the idealized objective or statement of ultimate purpose. This statement describes what we would hope to accomplish as a final end in the social action or public service program. Although such a formulation suggests neither a specific set of activities nor a timetable for execution, it does provide us with: (a) a theoretical reason for our program; (b) a fixed direction indicative of progress; and (c) a set of yardsticks which constitute the real standard against which all other measures of success must some day be validated. Nevertheless, despite the obvious significance of the *idealized* ultimate objectives, it is the *practical* immediate objectives which represent the translation from purpose to program, and which make public services possible. Most program evaluation consists essentially of the measurement of our success in reaching these practical objectives.

LEVELS OF OBJECTIVES

A distinction is often made between "objectives," "activities," and "steps" arranged in a descending order, with each of the latter terms used to denote action taken to implement a former one. In this sense, the objectives make up an ordered series, each of which is dependent for its existence upon an objective at the next higher level, while each is, in turn, implemented by means of lower-level objectives. In this framework there is a descending order of objectives, beginning with the idealized objective and ending, at the lowest level, with a subdivision of administrative tasks. In general, the staff officers assume responsibility for the higher-order objectives, with each of a succession of lower-ranked field workers being charged with one of the intermediate objectives on the descending scale.

Let us use a county dental health program as an illustration. The idealized, or ultimate, objective is the reduction of dental disease among all children in the county. A high-order intermediate objective for the health officer might be the provision of complete dental care for children through a combination of private dental care, school dental corrections, and topical fluoride. His dental director may adopt as his immediate objective the institution of dental clinics within the school system. The school dentist implements this, and his practical objective might be to achieve dental examinations and care for all of the first-grade children at the Central Avenue school. His dental hygienist, in turn, has the task of applying topical fluoride to the first-grade children's teeth after the dentist completes the operative work. Her assistant may be responsible for the objective of obtaining parental consent to all dental procedures. Evaluation studies may even be carried out at still lower levels than these, that is, how to write letters that bring consent or how to educate the parents so that they seek dental care for their child.

Program evaluation works back up this scale of objectives. After the degree to which an objective is met has been determined, this finding becomes a step toward the next higher objective. If each of the dental hygienists in our illustration does her job satisfactorily, this success contributes toward the total program for each school dentist. If each dentist does his job, the success of his program provides further progress toward the dental director's objective of complete dental care. The final evaluation of the entire dental program is then sought by the health officer in a reduction of the incidence of dental caries.

Much of the difficulty in communication about evaluation has occurred because of confusion among these different levels of objectives. Some evaluators have felt it sufficient to evaluate a training program by noting that the student has learned his lesson well. Others insist it must first be proven that this learning has actually resulted in the trainee doing a better job. According to the framework proposed here, both approaches are right, even though one may be more desirable than the other; they merely evaluate objectives at different levels.

Such subdivisions and classifications of objectives are highly arbitrary, depending upon both theoretical and administrative considerations. On the one hand, the present state of knowledge concerning the social problem, including the validity of the assumptions to be made at each stage of the process, will help to identify "logical" points of entry for control programs. However, advancing knowledge will greatly affect both assumptions and goals and today's intermediate objective may well become tomorrow's immediate objective. In addition, administrative factors such as personnel, funds, and facilities will often dictate how a program may be divided into subgoals corresponding to available resources and the assignment of separate administrative responsibility. That which is indicated logically on the basis of existing knowledge may have to give way to what is administratively feasible or even traditionally acceptable to both professionals and public.

Ordering the hierarchy of objectives according to the division of organizational responsibilities has been proposed by Rosenstock and Getting as the basis for a large-scale program of evaluative research. According to their framework, the division of labor in an organization is such that the technique or methods of work to be used at any level become the objectives of the immediately lower level. In turn, the objectives at any level form the methods of the immediately higher level. Thus, the functional relationship between any two contiguous levels is that of objective and method for achieving that objective. In this sense, any program can be divided into a chain of events in which each event is the result of the one that comes before it and a necessary condition to the one that comes after it. Evaluation then consists of validating the means-ends relationships between each adjacent pair comprising the program.[3]

One may move from the global evaluation of a total public service program or even department to segmental evaluations of their component parts. There is a strong tendency, however, to try to evaluate programs in terms of ultimate criteria of success rather than according to immediate or intermediate criteria. As Lemkau and Pasamanick point out in relation to mental health programs, "We have allowed our concepts to become obsessed by the idea of wholeness, devaluing any part-observations because they fall short of global understanding."[4] The idea of the interrelatedness of these various levels of evaluation is expressed by Herzog as one of movement "from the abstract to the concrete, from the whole to its parts, with the parts becoming ever more limited, specific," characterized by a paraphrase of the old jingle:

> Big criteria have little criteria upon their
>   backs to bite 'em.
> The small ones have still smaller, and so on
>   *ad infinitum.*[5]

This concept of a cumulative chain of objectives progressing from the most immediate practical objective toward the ultimate ideal goal is illustrated in the accompanying step-wise chart of different levels of evaluation for health educational literature. Greenberg and Mattison point out that "intermediate aims are based upon the postulate that morbidity and mortality will eventually be affected if a series or chain of prior accomplishments are fulfilled. They are not endpoints in themselves. . . . In terms of the ultimate objective, however, this kind of evaluation assumes that the literature will reach a large proportion of the population for whom it was intended, that it will be read, that it will have some effect (sooner or later, direct or indirect) in motivating the reader to carry out the recommended procedures, and that eventually a reduction in mortality will ensue."[6]

Reduction in morbidity or mortality.

Number or proportion of persons who are meeting prescribed and accepted standards.

Number or proportion of persons who change their patterns of behavior in accordance with the new knowledge. This may be verbalized, but is more accurate when observed in action.

Number or proportion of persons who change opinions or attitudes from the new knowledge.

Number or proportion of persons who learn the facts contained therein.

Number or proportion of persons who glance at or read it.

Number or proportion of persons who see the material.

Number or proportion of persons who receive the material.

Number of requests received for the material, or number distributed.

Number of pieces of literature available for distribution.

Pretesting of literature by special readability formulas.

The extent to which immediate and intermediate goals can be divorced from ultimate goals as valid in themselves poses a difficult question. Certainly there is a tremendous amount of activity, perhaps the largest proportion of all public service work, devoted to the successful attainment of immediate and intermediate goals which appear to have only a very indirect bearing upon ultimate goals.

MacMahon and his associates would distinguish between intermediate goals as an "evaluation of technic" and limit "evaluation of accomplishment" to ultimate goals only. The example they offer deals with surgery as a treatment for breast cancer. An evaluation of accomplishment would have to show that surgical removal of the affected breast leads to a lengthening of life among patients with breast cancer, while an evaluation of technic could be limited to the successful performance of the breast surgery itself. In an evaluation of technic, however, "cause and effect are not at issue." Given this distinction, an evaluation of technic in the absence of any evaluation of accomplishment becomes largely meaningless. "Unless it has been shown that the use of a certain technic is followed by beneficial results, what is the use of making sure that the technic is being followed?"[7]

Practically, there can be very little argument about this requirement that immediate and intermediate goals constitute valid steps toward the attainment of some ultimate goal. Otherwise activity becomes substituted for effect and the goals that lead to the adoption of certain means tend to be forgotten as the means become ends in and of themselves. However, knowledge is never complete and there must always be gaps in the "cause-effect" sequence which can only be filled by making assumptions concerning the validity of the intermediate steps. Thus, the validity assumptions discussed previously become the indispensable cement which binds the hierarchy of objectives together. The identification and examination of these assumptions according to confidence limits of validity becomes essential to our progress up the scale of objectives. Even the immediate objective most removed from the ultimate objective must theoretically at least be tied into a sequence of events which moves toward this ultimate objective. Such linkages are often, if not usually, taken for granted but upon challenge they must be reproducible.[8]

ASSUMPTIONS OF VALIDITY

An assumption of validity must be made whenever one moves from a higher-order objective to a lower one. Hence, every lower-level objective must assume *all* of the assumptions made for *all* of the objectives above it in the scale. Any program which is based upon a false set of major assumptions cannot be rescued by its lower-level objectives, although quite sound evaluations might still be done for each of these individually. It is possible to evaluate ways of making a pamphlet more readable, even if the facts in the reading matter are false. For example, it was quite feasible to show that mothers could be motivated to feed their babies on a rigid time schedule, even though today we believe this dictum wrong.

There are only two ways one can move up the scale of objectives in an evaluation: (a) by proving the intervening assumptions through research, that is, changing an assumption to a fact, or (b) by assuming their validity without full research proof. When the former is possible, we can then interpret our success in meeting a lower-level objective as automatic progress toward a higher one. Knowing the high potency of tetanus toxoid, we can equate a certain program of immunization to a given level of community immunity. Similarly, we can feel fairly sure that a one ppm sodium fluoride concentration in our water supply is a valid stimulus for a 60 per cent caries reduction among the children drinking it since birth.

When an assumption cannot be proved, we still must attempt to progress upward since few of us would wish to defend low-order objectives for their own sake. But we go upward at our peril. To a great extent, the ultimate worth of evaluation for public service programs will depend upon research proof of the validity of the assumptions involved in the establishment of key objectives.

Let us look at a program of tuberculosis control as an example of how assumptions may be handled.[9] The idealized objective is "the elimination of all morbidity and mortality from tuberculosis." Its chief assumptions are as follows:

(a) Man's life is worth prolonging. His productivity should be kept high as long as possible, and disease and suffering are to be avoided. This is a value assumption which requires justification only to a "man from Mars."

(b) The continued biologic existence of the tubercle bacillus is unnecessary and undesirable. Although partly a value assumption, this is also partly a validity assumption. It is possible that the eradication of tuberculosis could lead to circumstances which would be even more unfavorable for mankind. However, in the absence of such evidence, we must make the assumption.

(c) The total physical, social, and emotional cost of tuberculosis control will be less than that of the disease. This is another part value, part validity assumption, which we can restudy from time to time as our program proceeds.

The next lower level of objective might include: "The earliest possible detection and isolation of all cases of reinfection tuberculosis." Let us look at the assumptions of this objective:

(a) The disease spreads from infectious human cases to others and hence prompt detection and isolation of these cases will reduce tuberculosis incidence. This is a validity assumption which we will probably never test under controlled study conditions. As a matter of fact, we must admit that tuberculosis case and death rates have also fallen in many areas which have not had specific case finding and case control programs. Moreover, despite all of the years of mass x-ray effort, we still seem unable to improve appreciably the proportion of cases found to be in the early stage at the time of first diagnosis.

(b) Infectious cases may be discovered by modern techniques. This validity assumption has been proved as essentially correct as long as one is willing to note the problems of reliability which exist to a predictable degree if only one person reads the chest x-ray.

(c) A chest x-ray is a relatively harmless procedure. This assumption is being challenged by increasing knowledge about the effects of ionizing radiation.

A next lower order of objective would be: "The examination by x-ray of all contacts with known cases of tuberculosis." The chief assumption implied here is that this group not only has a higher incidence of infection than the average adult, but one sufficiently higher to justify its being singled out for special follow-up. The truth of this assumption may vary from area to area and from time to time. The problem becomes more complicated if we try to compute the changing relative priority of contact examinations in case-finding with, for example, the examination of old cured cases, inmates of nursing homes, jails, or general hospitals.

The next level of case-finding objectives brings us finally to immediate, practical goals: "At least one x-ray examination on all (or 80 per cent if one wishes to set administrative levels of practicality) of the contacts with cases of reportable tuberculosis, and one such examination per year thereafter for those remaining in contact with active cases." Now we have finally arrived at what we commonly recognize as a "standard of recommended practice." If we wish this standard to be considered as a true expression of the idealized objective "the elimination of tuberculosis," we must remember the crucial significance of each of the assumptions we have made so far. In addition, we have made a new assumption in establishing the present objective or standard, namely, that this specific procedure is the most valid, reliable, efficient, and adequate method for detecting these particular tuberculosis cases.[10]

When one considers all of the assumptions that have been made, it is not difficult to feel unsure and easily dissatisfied with the final standard. This is all to the good, since such insecurities lead to a frequent restudy of the problem, a healthy sharing of experience with other workers perhaps proceeding on other assumptions, and further refinements of the standard.

Let us emphasize again that if one of the key assumptions of our higher objectives is proved wrong, the standard must inevitably collapse. If, for example, the chest x-ray were found to be a significantly harmful procedure, or if tuberculosis disease in a future era becomes largely endobronchial in site and could not then be detected by x-ray, then our illustrative standard would be meaningless. These are not far-fetched possibilities. Concern with ionizing radiation has already had an impact upon the frequency of the chest x-ray examination of certain groups in the community.

The level of objective which one chooses to evaluate will also determine the scope or generalizability of one's findings. The higher the level of objective, the larger the number of activities that are evaluated. One may characterize studies of high-level objectives as having higher "evaluative" power than those of low-level objectives. Such studies cover more events and become generalizable to a greater variety of actions. Such generalizability is, of course, related to the underlying assumptions at each level of evaluation with the assumptions themselves acquiring a higher level of theoretical importance as one moves up the scale from practical to ideal objectives. Part of the greater significance of evaluative research at a higher level of objective also stems from the fact that the higher the "evaluative" power of a study, the larger the number of possibilities for its being proven ineffective. Effectiveness at the top of the scale, generally subsumes effectiveness at lower levels.

Hovland implies this principle when he discusses the greater significance of evaluative research which aims at the testing of variables or principles rather than specific products or programs.[11] Generalizations from one specific program evaluation to another program are strongly limited. However, an evaluation study which tests the effectiveness of an approach or principle of action, in the course of evaluating the specific activity or service, may have both wider theoretical and practical relevance. We shall examine this aspect of evaluative research in more detail in the chapters on methodology when we discuss the problem of establishing "causal" connections between one's actions and the measured effects.

CATEGORIES OF EVALUATION

In addition to varying levels of objectives, evaluative research may be conducted in terms of different categories of effect. These categories represent the various criteria of success or failure according to which a program may be evaluated. They may be applied to any level of objective and serve to define the type of measure to be used in judging an activity.

Several classifications have been proposed for ordering the different types of criteria. Paul speaks of three major sets of criteria: (1) *assessment of effort,* by which is meant the energy and action of the service team, that is, talks given, visits made, meetings attended, patients seen; (2) *assessment of effect,* which refers to the results of the effort rather than the effort itself, that is, changes in health information, attitudes, or behavior, reduction in incidence of disease; and (3) *assessment of process,* which deals with an analysis of why and how an effect was achieved, that is, resistance of community leaders, lack of motivation among potential clients, cultural superstition, and fear.[12]

The distinction between effort and effect is one which appears again and again in the evaluation literature. Whether a public service program can be established (effort) is quite a different question from whether it does any good (effect). As Kandle points out, "A tremendous part of our dollars, staff time and activity in evaluation is still in terms of effort. Many reports, papers, surveys, evaluations, etc., are still written and thought of only in terms of personnel, hospital beds, visits of patients, slides examined or good intentions proclaimed. We still do not have many practical indices of accomplishments."[13]

Obviously, it is much less difficult to evaluate effort than effect. In terms of the hierarchy of objectives discussed previously, effort would come low on the scale, representing one's immediate objective of establishing services. Effect, on the other hand, would represent a much higher order of objective, involving many more assumptions and being much less subject to definitive proof. As described by James and his associates, "Ideally, the final standard will be an expression of public health accomplishment. Such standards will be in terms of patients restored to health, active cases discovered, children immunized, and environmental hazards corrected. In the meantime, we may have to accept standards of "work effort," such as patient-days of hospital care, nursing visits, clinic visits and sanitation inspections."[14]

An additional distinction is made by Wright in terms of effects, effectiveness, and efficiency. Effects refer to the ultimate influence of a program upon a target population. Effectiveness focuses not on final results but on the ability of the program to be carried out successfully. Efficiency adds an additional criterion related to Paul's assessment of process; namely, how well and at what cost was the program conducted relative to other ways of producing a similar effect.[15]

In general, we would like to propose five categories of criteria according to which the success or failure of a program may be evaluated. These are: (1) *Effort,* (2) *Performance,* (3) *Adequacy of Performance,* (4) *Efficiency,* and (5) *Process.* These categories are interrelated with an evaluation of effort and performance necessarily preceding one of adequacy, efficiency or process. Furthermore, in general, successful performance implies successful effort, although such performance may still be inadequate in terms of the total problem being attacked, or inefficient as compared to some alternative method.

Let us look briefly at each of these categories in turn:[16]

1. *Effort.* Evaluations in this category have as their criterion of success the quantity and quality of activity that takes place. This represents an assessment of input or energy regardless of output. It is intended to answer the questions "What did you do" and "How well did you do it?"

Yardsticks in this category are based either on the capacity for effort or the effort itself. Effort evaluation assumes that the specific activity is a valid means of reaching higher goals. This is usually the easiest type of evaluation; it is easier to maintain administrative records than to measure success of efforts. Although effort evaluation does not give key answers, it can be valuable. At least it indicates that something is being done in an attempt to meet a problem. Certainly this is a necessary if not sufficient condition for accomplishment. As Paul states, "If figures show that an agency is inactive, it can fairly well be inferred that little good is being accomplished in the way of health promotion."[17] As a matter of fact, the best currently available measure of the adequacy of local public services is a very general capacity-to-serve measure: the presence of a sufficient number of specific kinds of qualified personnel.

Evaluation at this level has been compared to the measurement of the number of times a bird flaps his wings without any attempt to determine how far the bird has flown. If we were to take 100,000 chest x-rays of chronically ill patients admitted to general hospitals, we would find a good number of cases of tuberculosis. If, on the other hand, we took a similar number of films of children admitted to kindergarten, we would find very few cases of re-infection type of tuberculosis. Evaluations by counting public health nursing visits to patients, by counting persons attending health department clinics, by counting the amount of money spent for a given health program are all examples of evaluation of effort.

2. *Performance.* Performance or effect criteria measure the results of effort rather than the effort itself. This requires a clear statement of one's objective. How much is accomplished relative to an immediate goal? Did any change occur? Was the change the one intended? Performance can be measured at several levels: the number of cases found, number hospitalized, number cured or rehabilitated. Performance standards often involve key validity assumptions; however, in general, evaluation of performance involves fewer assumptions than evaluation of effort.

The ultimate justification of a public service or community action program in seeking public support must rest with the proof of its effectiveness in alleviating the problem being attacked. For example, a venereal disease clinic is established to decrease the incidence of venereal disease through diagnosis and treatment. The proof of its validity must lie in fewer cases of venereal disease than would be true in the absence of such clinics. This can be compared to measuring how far the bird has flown instead of merely counting the flappings of his wings as was done in the previous discussion. When performance is evaluated, one studies how many cases of tuberculosis were found by the x-ray program, how many children were immunized in child health conferences, how many cancer cases were found, treated, and cured in cancer detection clinics.

Paul describes the example of a mental health program which rated an A for effort, but was a failure in terms of performance.[18] A team of psychiatrists, sociologists, and social workers introduced an intensive campaign to change public attitudes toward the mentally ill. Motion pictures, pamphlets, special books placed in the library, radio broadcasts, public speakers, small group discussions—the whole armamentarium of health education was skillfully applied. The cooperation of influential people—editors, civic leaders, educators, physicians—was successfully obtained. But a comparison of the results of this effort with that of a control community in which nothing was done provided a good measure of effect—virtually zero. The evaluation was a success, but there was no change to be measured.[19]

Performance evaluation can be made at several levels. It could be, for example, the number of cases of tuberculosis found after x-ray, the number of these cases hospitalized, or the number of them cured after hospitalization. While not generally recognized, there are a number of key validity assumptions involved in most evaluations of performance. The fact that a large number of people are reported as having received services does not ensure that all of these services were given properly and were truly completed.

Problems of reliability are also extremely important in performance ratings or standards, and must be taken into consideration. For example, the proportion of diabetics diagnosed in a case-finding program will vary according to the blood sugar test used, the age groups tested, the time elapsed after the last meal, and the follow-up procedures used. Hence each performance standard devised should specify all significant modifying conditions.

3. *Adequacy of Performance.* This criterion of success refers to the degree to which effective performance is adequate to the total amount of need. Thus, a program of intensive psychotherapy for a small group of mentally ill individuals may show highly effective results, but as a public health measure prove thoroughly inadequate to meet the problem of mental illness in an entire community. Adequacy is obviously a relative measure, depending upon how high one sets one's goals. A polio control program to be effective may set a goal of 80 per cent immunization, but a much lower percentage might suffice for an influenza program.

A measure of adequacy tells us how effective a program has been in terms of the denominator of total need. Although accurate data describing the unmet need are not generally available, some estimates have been made that are useful. The National Tuberculosis Association has estimated the total unknown cases of tuberculosis in the United States, and the American Diabetes Association the number of those with unrecognized diabetes. The National Health Survey is expected to supply much valuable data on unmet needs for various disabling illnesses. It should be recognized that the idealized objective is an expression that always includes the adequacy concept.

One fairly common index of adequacy consists of measuring the impact of one's program in terms of the rate of effectiveness multiplied by the number of people exposed to the program. For example, if we have a program which is 50 per cent effective, and apply it to only 1,000 people, the impact will be felt by 500 people. However, a program which can be applied to 10,000 cases and which is only 10 per cent effective will still have an impact on 1,000 people. In other words, if a program has a high potency, but low exposure, total impact may not be great. This point was well made by Bigman in evaluating the effectiveness of religious programs: "In the first place, the *number of persons* may be so small as to render the program relatively ineffective. Here we must distinguish between effectiveness and *impact*. By the latter term I mean the strength of the influence upon exposed individuals. A program or activity may have considerable impact, affecting markedly the thoughts and actions of those it touches; it will be necessarily judged ineffective if it is so designed that this impact is confined to a small fraction of the group it is intended to reach and influence."[20]

To continue the analogy made in reference to effort and performance, one would like to measure how far the bird has flown in terms of where he has to go. It is sobering to realize, for example, that the mass survey chest x-ray program, despite its publicity and emphasis, is finding only 10 to 15 per cent of the new cases of tuberculosis which are reported each year. The remainder of these cases are still being reported by private physicians, and many of them not until the disease has progressed to a late stage.

The criterion of adequacy needs to be tempered by a realistic awareness of what is possible at any given state of knowledge and available resources. There is a tendency in service programs to think in terms of total effectiveness. Much less ambitious ultimate goals must be set, in general, for judging adequacy. The notion of increments of progress toward the "idealized" objective has to be built into the concept of adequacy, as is currently being advocated for social case work.

4. *Efficiency.* A positive answer to the question, "Does it work?" often gives rise to a follow-up question, "Is there any better way to attain the same results?" Efficiency is concerned with the evaluation of alternative paths or methods in terms of costs—in money, time, personnel, and public convenience. In a sense, it represents a ratio between effort and performance—output divided by input. As defined in the *Glossary of Administrative Terms in Public Health,* efficiency is "the capacity of an individual, organization, facility, operation, or activity to produce results in proportion to the effort expended."[21]

In the steadily increasing competition for public funds among all public services, the criteria of efficiency are coming more and more to dominate the evaluation picture. As health, education, and welfare plan and develop better services, a major decision has to be one of priorities, both between these services and, within each field of service, among the various possible programs. In an age of rapid scientific advances, more is

known than is being applied and one of the basic criteria for evaluating
that which is being applied is its relative worth compared to alternative
approaches.[22]

Few programs can be justified at all cost and a measure of efficiency
needs to be incorporated into evaluative research whenever possible. Employing again the now familiar bird analogy, it is like asking the questions:
"Could the bird have arrived at his destination more efficiently by some
other means than flying the way he did? Did he take advantage of air cur-
rents; did he fly too high or not high enough?"

The emphasis on efficiency is closely related to attempts at streamlining
traditional programs. Many programs were justified on the basis of evaluative research made many years ago and new developments require periodic reevaluations of continued efficiency. Can the same end result be
achieved in different ways and at less cost? Can less skilled personnel substitute adequately for physicians, nurses, and sanitary engineers? For example, new technical developments may make it safe to use relatively untrained personnel. Can self-inspection programs achieve as effective a
degree of control? After an initial period of growth, less rigorous formal
controls may be possible. Such questions point out that standards of performance will be improved if they consider the effort-costs involved and
arrive at comparative efficiency ratings.[23]

Efficiency criteria are highly significant, for example, for many of the
public health decisions made in chronic disease programs. Any new test
for mass screening requires careful attention to the number of false
positives which will occur. "Positive" cases usually must be followed up
by elaborate and costly examination procedures. A screening program
which produces too large a number of false positives could rapidly over-
whelm the follow-up mechanisms of a community. Thus, techniques
which give a high proportion of false positives may have to be discarded
for mass use. A history of chest pain as an indication of coronary heart disease, the measurement of obesity as an index of hypertension, the presence of low gastric acidity as a warning sign for incipient cancer of the
stomach are all clinical screening tests which have not been widely applied to mass detection programs because of their high number of false
positives. For this reason the Commission on Chronic Illness has listed the
criteria for the evaluation of screening tests and mass screening programs
as: (a) the reliability of the test; (b) the validity of the test, including
an analysis of true positives, true negatives, false positives, and false negatives; (c) yield of a screening program; (d) cost; and (e) acceptance.[24]

Since World War II an enormous amount of attention has been paid to a new field called Operations Research. Through an interdisciplinary approach, the operations research team sets up a representative model of a program in order to make high probability predictions that certain events will occur if specific recommendations are followed. As defined by Ackoff, the basic purpose of Operations Research is "to determine which alternative course of action is most effective (optimum) relative to the decision-maker's set of pertinent objectives."[25] The practitioner need not feel obligated to follow the recommendations derived from Operations Research. Rarely can all of the factors upon which the decision depends be made part of the theoretical model. Yet, through this technique, the degree of understanding of the problem based upon probable fact can be increased, and the use of the scientific method extended farther into the realm of administrative decision. Operations Research is a valuable means of evaluating and improving the efficiency of public service programs.

5. *Process.* In the course of evaluating the success or failure of a program, a great deal can be learned about how and why a program works or does not work. Strictly speaking, this analysis of the process whereby a program produces the results it does, is not an inherent part of evaluative research. An evaluation study may limit its data collection and analysis simply to determining whether or not a program is successful according to the preceding four criteria without examining the why's and wherefor's of this success or failure. However, an analysis of process can have both administrative and scientific significance, particularly where the evaluation indicates that a program is *not* working as expected. Locating the cause of the failure may result in modifying the program so that it will work, instead of its being discarded as a complete failure.

Paul points to three circumstances which permitted an analysis of process in connection with the unsuccessful community mental health program mentioned previously. "For one thing, project personnel conducted a series of intensive interviews before and after the educational campaign. . . . For another, they took note of the changing reception they received. . . . Furthermore, they used a social science frame of reference to 'make sense' of the evidence they collected and observed."[26]

"Making sense" of the evaluative findings is the basic reason for adding a concern with process to the evaluation study. Otherwise one is left with the descriptive results of the evaluation, but without any explanations. In the following chapters, we will discuss this use of evaluative research in more detail in terms of establishing a "causal" connection between what was done and the results that were obtained.

The analysis of process may be made according to four main dimensions dealing with: (1) the attributes of the program itself; (2) the population exposed to the program; (3) the situational context within which the program takes place; and (4) the different kinds of effects produced by the program. We may view this analysis in terms of the specification of each of these four dimensions as follows:

1. Specification of the *attributes* of the program that make it more or less successful. This type of evaluation attempts to diagnose specific causes of success or failure within the program itself. It requires a breakdown of the component parts of the program and the identification of those aspects which contribute to or detract from the overall effect of the program. It may happen, for example, that a poor appointment system may negate the otherwise successful operation of a clinic program.

2. Specification of *the recipients* of the program who are more or less affected. Which people are most affected by the program? Whom do you succeed in reaching and whom don't you reach? Who makes the best target population for a program—the individual, the group, the public? As end product or as influencer of others?

3. Specification of the *conditions* under which the program is more or less successful: locale, timing, auspices, and so on. Could the same remedial reading clinic set up in a different place under different conditions be more or less or equally successful?

4. Specification of the *effects* produced by the program. What aspects of the final results are you going to use as your criteria of judgment? For example, effects could be broken down in the following ways:

(a) Unitary or multiple effects
(b) Unintentional or side-effects
(c) Duration of effects
(d) Type of effect
    (1) cognitive
    (2) attitudinal
    (3) behavioral

Recognition of the importance of such questions in evaluative research is given by the World Health Organization in its analysis of methods of evaluation for international assistance projects. Answers to the following questions provide the background against which "the accomplishments of a project may be evaluated."

> What are the specific social changes being sought? . . . What are the conditions in the project area to which a project must be adjusted if it is to attract the active support of the people? What are the chan-

nels of social communication that permit the flow of education from those responsible for the project to the people and—what is too seldom stressed—a flow of the attitudes and responses of the people to those responsible for the project? What are the social barriers, so often loosely classified as "superstitions," that must be overcome if the project is to achieve its objectives? Who are the leaders—government, family, religious—whose decisions determine support of or resistance to the project, its methods and its expansion?[27]

Obviously, the number and extent to which these specifications are included in an evaluation study will depend upon the statement of objective, the research resources available, and administrative support. In effect, seeking answers to the questions raised by these specifications indicates the potential research character of program evaluation. Such an approach combines evaluation with research and attempts to make a contribution to basic knowledge as well as to administrative decision-making. To complete our analogy to the bird, it is as if we tried to learn something about the anatomy of the bird or the principles of flight as a further step toward understanding its effort, performance, adequacy, and efficiency.

The following illustration, taken from an outline for the evaluation of tuberculosis programs prepared by James, summarizes these five criteria, including an analysis of underlying validity assumptions, for three different levels of a tuberculosis control program representing long-range, intermediate, and immediate objectives.[28]

I. *Long-Range Objectives*
   A. *The earliest possible detection and isolation of all cases of re-infection tuberculosis.*
      (1) *Assumptions*
         a. The disease spreads from infectious cases to others. Outside of relatively minor sources such as unpasteurized milk, prompt control of the infectious case will prevent spread. Although this assumption is generally considered proved, there is evidence that tuberculosis mortality has decreased even in the absence of effective community programs for detection and isolation. Perhaps other factors, such as general standard of living, are even more important than the isolation of infectious persons.
         b. Infectious cases may be discovered by modern technics. Generally proved—all but a very few will be found by current detection methods, but there are still problems such as: lack of agreement between various x-ray readers and use of various standards for sputum analysis and diagnosis of activity. These can affect the validity and reliability of the yardsticks.

(2) *Categories of Evaluation*
   a. *Effort*—Physician man-hours, nursing visits, x-rays, laboratory tests, clinic visits, etc., used in case-finding. Trends during past years for all of these.
   b. *Performance*—Yield of new cases by these various efforts, and trends during past years.
   c. *Adequacy*—Changes in the unmet need indicating success such as: (1) decreased proportion of cases first reported by death certificate, (2) increased proportion of cases found in the early stages, (3) decreased prevalence of positive tuberculins and clinical tuberculosis among contacts of newly discovered active cases, (4) increased proportion of cases found in those special groups among which cases are believed to be more prevalent.
   d. *Efficiency*—Could effort have been more productive in tuberculosis control if partly or wholly applied to isolation, hospitalization, treatment, field supervision, rehabilitation or known cases, and preventive methods using BCG?
   e. *Process*—Relative success of different aspects of program, i.e., nursing vs. clinic visits. Attributes of program components producing difficulty. Resistance of different population segments. Negative side-effects.

II. *Intermediate Objectives*

A. *Isolation by prompt hospitalization of all infectious cases until rendered noninfectious.*
   (1) *Assumptions:*
   Home treatment with antituberculosis drugs is not sufficient for prevention of further spread. The hospital patient is taught how to conduct himself; hence he is made more "noninfectious" even if at discharge he still has a positive sputum. Both of these assumptions require further proof. Studies of the value of antituberculosis drugs as an alternate procedure to hospitalization are under way. More could be done to show whether the formerly hospitalized active patient is able to prevent spread to his familial contacts. This could be done by selected tuberculin studies.
   (2) *Categories of Evaluation*
   a. *Effort*—Total man-hours, nurse visits, patient days, etc. required to get patients admitted, maintained in hospital, taught various things, and given treatments.
   b. *Performance*—Number of cases discharged as improved, cured, against medical advice, worse, or dead. Time between diagnosis and first nursing visit, between diagnosis and admission, number of active cases hospitalized and number never hospitalized.

      c. *Adequacy*—Proportion of active cases hospitalized and never hospitalized. Proportion of cases discharged under various categories with trend during past years. Proportion of those admitted within one month of diagnosis as active case. Proportion who stay at least 90 days after admission. Are preventable factors present which delay admission or shorten the duration of hospital care?

      d. *Efficiency*—How has the length of hospitalization changed during modern times? Is the hospital being used most efficiently now, or do we need a new look at the relationship between home and hospital treatment?

      e. *Process*—Relative effectiveness of different approaches to secure cooperation of hospitalized patient. Which individuals make the best patients? Which hospitals are most successful? Why?

III. *Immediate Objectives*

  A. Provision of appropriate x-ray facilities for general hospitals and encouragement of the use of existing facilities for the x-raying of all adult admissions. As a more practical early objective we may seek to obtain the cooperation of 50 per cent of our hospitals and expect them to x-ray 80 per cent of their adult admissions.

    (1) *Assumptions*

      a. Patients coming to hospitals constitute a group of high enough risk to justify giving them special attention. Also that it is easier to reach these groups in hospitals than elsewhere. This assumption requires constant proof in view of the changing picture of tuberculosis and the improvement in the efficiency of x-ray programs for the general adult population.

      b. Screening for tuberculosis by use of x-ray involves assumptions as to the validity and reliability of this technique.

    (2) *Categories of Evaluation*

      a. *Effort*—Number of films taken, proportion of all hospitals participating in survey, proportion of admissions in participating hospitals actually x-rayed. Proportion of screened positives followed up with additional examinations.

      b. *Performance*—Yield of new confirmed cases in hospitals in rural areas, small and large cities. Yield of other pathology. Yield for each age-sex group of hospital admissions.

      c. *Adequacy*—Total cases screened in terms of total potential: (1) in participating hospitals, and (2) all

> hospitals in the area. Total new cases found in terms of total unknown cases estimated in the area.
>
> d. *Efficiency*—Considering the total number of new cases confirmed per film taken:
>
> (1) Would the x-raying of other groups have been more productive of new cases?
>
> (2) Was the confirmation rate so low that the program is inefficient?
>
> (3) Are the right age groups being x-rayed to uncover new cases?
>
> (4) Are hospitals using the equipment sufficiently to justify the expense of the program?
>
> (5) Are a sufficient number of the cases discovered new cases, or are they persons already known?
>
> (6) Could the cases have been discovered with less effort through any other method?
>
> e. *Process*—Under what conditions and in what situations does hospital x-raying proceed most effectively? Why? Among which groups? Are there any unintended negative consequences to patient? Do x-rays reveal any other conditions?

This process of stating objectives, in terms of ultimate, intermediate, or immediate goals, of examining the underlying assumptions, and of setting up criteria of effort, performance, adequacy, efficiency, and process constitutes the basic procedure to be followed in conducting an evaluation study. In principle, this is what we mean by evaluative research. The following chapters will discuss, first, the methodological and then, the administrative considerations involved in putting these principles into practice.

N O T E S   T O   C H A P T E R   I V

1. *First National Conference on Evaluation in Public Health.* School of Public Health, University of Michigan, Ann Arbor, 1955, p. 21. As described by Smith: "Most programmes will be found to have more than one objective. The first step in conducting an evaluation is thus to achieve consensus among those responsible for the programme as to the order of priority of these multiple objectives. As part of the same process, it is helpful to analyze the more general and far-reaching objectives into steps or subgoals through which the programme seeks to achieve them. Often it may be found that achievement of specific and subgoals can be measured,

while the less tangible ultimate goals (international understanding, for instance) remain inaccessible." Smith, M. Brewster, "Evaluation of Exchange of Person," *International Social Science Bulletin*, vol. 7, no. 3, UNESCO, 1955, p. 389.

2. Herzog, Elizabeth, *Some Guide Lines for Evaluative Research*. U.S. Department of Health, Education, and Welfare, Children's Bureau, Washington, 1959, pp. 79–80.

3. Getting, Vlado A., and others, "Research in Evaluation in Public Health Practices." Paper presented at the 92nd Annual Meeting of the American Public Health Association, New York, October 5, 1964.

4. Lemkau, Paul V., and Benjamin Pasamanick, "Problems in Evaluation of Mental Health Programs," *American Journal of Orthopsychiatry*, vol. 27, January, 1957, pp. 55–58.

5. Herzog, Elizabeth, *op. cit.*, p. 17.

6. Greenberg, Bernard G., and Berwyn F. Mattison, "The Whys and Wherefores of Program Evaluation," *Canadian Journal of Public Health*, vol. 46, July, 1955, pp. 295–296.

7. MacMahon, Brian, Thomas F. Pugh, and George B. Hutchison, "Principles in the Evaluation of Community Mental Health Programs, "*American Journal of Public Health*, vol. 51, July, 1961, p. 964.

8. It is possible, of course, to move one's ultimate objective from the public service field to some other socially valued area, such as economic gain. In this case, immediate activity may be justified in terms of the increased employment of service workers. However, our concern here will be limited to "legitimate" service goals.

9. This example was developed by George James.

10. There is a special assumption involved whenever we pick a goal which is less than 100 per cent of approved practice. We are, of course, implying that the group not reached is substantially similar to the group reached.

11. Hovland, Carl I., Arthur A. Lumsdaine, and Fred D. Sheffield, *Experiments in Mass Communication*. Princeton University Press, Princeton, N.J., 1949.

12. Paul, Benjamin D., "Social Science in Public Health," *American Journal of Public Health*, vol. 46, November, 1956, pp. 1390–1396.

13. Kandle, Roscoe P., "The Need and Place of Evaluation in Public Health," *First National Conference on Evaluation in Public Health*, University of Michigan, 1955, p. 17.

14. James, George, Daniel Klepak, and Herman E. Hilleboe, "Fiscal Research in Public Health," *American Journal of Public Health*, vol. 45, July, 1955, p. 914.

15. Wright, Charles R., "Evaluating Mass Media Campaigns," *International Social Science Bulletin*, vol. 7, no. 3, 1955.

16. These categories were first presented by James in "Evaluation and Planning of Health Programs," *Administration of Community Health Services*, International City Managers' Association, Chicago, 1961, pp. 126–218. They are revised and expanded in this presentation.

17. Paul, Benjamin D., *op. cit.*, p. 1391.
18. *Ibid.*, pp. 1391–1392.
19. A fairly common mistake in evaluative research is to confuse the failure of the program with that of the evaluation study. An evaluation study which fails to show any effect can be quite successful as an evaluation—it was the program which was unsuccessful. It is, of course, possible that the evaluation measures were not sensitive enough, or even incorrectly chosen, to show an effect, but, given a carefully conducted study, the burden of proof rests upon the program itself.
20. Bigman, Stanley K., "Evaluating the Effectiveness of Religious Programs," *Review of Religious Research*, vol. 2, Winter, 1961, p. 113.
21. "Glossary of Administrative Terms in Public Health," *American Journal of Public Health*, vol. 50, February, 1960, p. 226.
22. The possible conflict between "scientific" and "efficiency" standards in evaluation is described by James and his colleagues as follows: "Health administrators may believe that the approach to the problem of standards in public health should first be made on a scientific basis before one becomes concerned about the fiscal aspects of the problem. Since health officers are now dealing routinely with fiscal authorities in order to obtain funds, practical considerations dictate that this problem be approached from the financial side." James, George, and others, *op. cit.*, pp. 913–914.
23. An interesting example of "efficiency" as a criterion in the evaluation of a mass x-ray program is provided by a study which attempted to evaluate the relative efficiency of different types of location placements for the x-ray machines. Gurin, Gerald, and Charles A. Metzner, *Target Bronx*, Bureau of Public Health Economics, School of Public Health, University of Michigan, Research Series No. 7, Ann Arbor, October, 1957.
24. *Proceedings of the Conference on the Preventive Aspects of Chronic Illness*, Chicago, March 12–14, 1951, pp. 64–67.
25. Ackoff, Russell L., "The Development of Operations Research as a Science," *Operations Research*, vol. 4, June, 1956, pp. 265–295. This article contains an excellent bibliography on operations research.
26. Paul, Benjamin D., *op. cit.*, p. 1392. The major explanation concerned the defensive reactions of an uninformed public—apathy followed by antagonism—toward a threat to their safe and customary view of people as sane or insane.
27. *Organizational Study on Programme Analysis and Evaluation.* World Health Organization, Geneva, Switzerland, January 8, 1954, p. 40.
28. James, George, *Outline for the Evaluation of Tuberculosis Programs.* Department of Health, Akron, Ohio. Mimeographed, n.d.

The Conduct of Evaluative Research

By and large, evaluation studies of action or service programs are notably deficient in both research design and execution. Examples of evaluative research which satisfy even the most elementary tenets of the scientific method are few and far between. An attempt by an Evaluation Planning Group in Mental Health to approach evaluation as an experiment in social change concluded that *no* situations could be found which satisfied the three basic elements of a "meaningful evaluation of mental health demonstrations":

1. The existence of a presumption that a particular set of activities reduces the frequency of a specific group of morbidities.
2. The ability to provide the study population with the particular set of activities concerned.
3. The existence of techniques which will permit measuring changes in the frequency of morbidities affected by the activities in question.[1]

The difficulty of applying the principles and techniques of scientific research to evaluation studies results from both logical and administrative factors. Much of the confusion and controversy over evaluation today may be traced to a failure to recognize certain inherent differences between the objectives and research conditions of evaluative as opposed to nonevaluative or so-called "basic" research. It is only too easy for professional critics of evaluation studies to "stand in the wings with knives sharpened, awaiting studies yet unborn,"[2] just as it is equally tempting for the evaluator to plead, "we cannot stand still for sophisticated research when cruder methods will provide the answers needed."[3]

The crucial issue is not simply one of "right" versus "wrong," not of "objectivity" versus "subjectivity," nor even of "standards" versus "expediency," but a rather complex mixture of differing values, purposes, and resources. Toward a better understanding of this problem, first, we examine the logical differences between evaluative and nonevaluative research, and, second, analyze the administrative situations within which these two types of research are conducted.

Evaluative research is a specific form of applied research whose primary goal is not the discovery of knowledge but rather a testing of the application of knowledge. A great deal has been written about the differences between applied and basic research, taken as opposite poles of a continuum ranging from "pure" research to "engineering" research.[4] While much of this controversy is more vituperative than productive, and while a great deal, if not most, research has both basic and applied elements, there can be little question about the fundamental differences between the two, especially at the extreme ends of the continuum. Confusion of the two underlies much of the heated debate over the "invalidity" of evaluative research or the "uselessness" of basic research.

In a general way, we may compare evaluative and nonevaluative research according to differing accents of both objectives and methods. In terms of objectives, evaluative research is more likely to be aimed at achieving some practical goal—its major emphasis is upon utility. The research, if successful, should provide helpful information for program planning, development, or operation. As described by Fleck, "The distinguishing feature converting a search for knowledge into an evaluation project is the presence of a purpose that the knowledge sought is to be used as a guide for practical action."[5]

In contrast, nonevaluative research, while it may have practical implications, is primarily aimed at increased understanding rather than manipulation or action. A basic research project has as its major objective the search for new knowledge regardless of the value of such knowledge for producing social change. The emphasis is upon studying the interrelationships of variables rather than upon the ability of man to influence these relationships through controlled intervention.[6]

A corollary of this distinction between understanding versus manipulation relates to contrasting degrees of abstraction versus specificity. Basic research aims at the formulation of theoretical generalizations or abstract predictions, while applied research stresses action in a highly specified situation involving concrete forecasts. Merton points out the following consequences of the restriction of applied research to concrete situations:

> (a) Every applied research must include some speculative inquiry into the role of diverse factors which can only be roughly assessed, not meticulously studied.

(b) The validity of the concrete forecast depends upon the degree of (noncompensated) error in any phase of the total inquiry. The weakest links in the chain of applied research may typically consist of the estimates of contingent conditions under which the investigated variables will in fact operate.

(c) To this degree, the recommendations for policy do not flow directly and exclusively from the research. Recommendations are the product of the research and the estimates of contingent conditions, these estimates not being of the same order of probability or precision as the more abstract interrelations examined in the research itself.

(d) Such contingencies make for indeterminacy of the recommendations derived from the research and thus create a gap between research and policy.[7]

Hyman distinguishes three types of research studies: (1) the theoretical or experimental, (2) the evaluative or programmatic, and (3) the diagnostic. The theoretical study emphasizes the testing of specific hypotheses relevant to some larger body of theory, while the evaluative study is designed to test the practical value of some action program; the diagnostic study explores some unknown, novel problem.[8] A similar distinction is made by Zetterberg who differentiates between *diagnosis* as leading to *descriptive studies* aimed at the development of *taxonomies*, and *explanation* which requires *verificational studies* whose purpose is to *test hypotheses*.[9] We would propose extending these typologies to *evaluation* involving *demonstration studies* with the objective of measuring *effectiveness*.

As one moves from the theoretical study to the evaluative study, the number of variables over which one has control decreases appreciably, while the number of contingent factors increases. These contingencies which surround any evaluative research project are an inherent aspect of the required specificity of the evaluation process and provide a major source of criticism for "basic" researchers accustomed to more rigid controls of extraneous factors. The concreteness of evaluative research as compared to the more abstract nonevaluative research raises some significant questions concerning the "meaning" of the data collected in both types of studies. The concept is the primary variable of interest in basic research; it is translatable into observable units, but these data remain only operational indices of the underlying concept and their worth derives from their ability to represent this concept reliably and validly. In evaluative research, on the other hand, the observable and measurable indices are *the* phenomena of interest; the action program usually is aimed directly at changing the values of these specific measures, and only indirectly at the underlying concept.

Hovland recognizes this problem when he discusses the difference between "program" and "variable" testing in evaluative research.[10] Program evaluation refers to the test of a total product with the purely practical objective of determining whether exposure to the program was accompanied by certain desired effects. Variable testing, on the other hand, is concerned with singling out specific components of the program, *as indices of some more generalizable stimuli,* and testing the effectiveness of these variables. Program testing has almost no generalizability, being applicable solely to the specific program being evaluated. Generalizations (to other products, populations, times) "have the status of untested hypotheses."

This is a major reason why so many evaluation studies appear repetitive —one can never be certain that a program which works in one situation will work in another. To the extent that evaluative research can focus upon the general variables underlying a specific program and test the effects of these variables rather than the effectiveness of the program as a whole, it may hope to produce findings of greater general significance.

An example may help to illustrate this point. An evaluation of the effectiveness of a prenatal clinic may be set up on a program basis by establishing the clinic according to some administrative design and then determining the number of mothers who attend. Such an evaluation may enable one to decide whether or not to continue this specific clinic but it will have only limited value for planning similar clinics in different areas or for different populations. However, if the clinic is established to test some specific action principle or variable, for example, the relative effectiveness of personal versus formal appeals for attendance, the results would have greater transferability to other situations. In this sense one might argue for the greater ultimate "practicality" of variable as opposed to program testing because of its stronger potential for generalization and accumulated knowledge.

This point is particularly relevant to the evaluation of demonstration projects. If the demonstration project is set up on a program-testing basis, then it is essential that the project approximate as closely as possible the realistic operating conditions under which similar programs would have to be set up on a wider scale, should the demonstration prove successful. Yet this is seldom the case. Most demonstration projects are established under as ideal conditions as possible to show not the feasibility of the proposed program so much as its potentiality. While this may be desirable as a means of gaining support for the program, it leaves unanswered the question of whether such programs can be successfully established under other than ideal conditions. It would seem desirable to differentiate between demonstration projects which are to serve as prototypes for actual operating programs and demonstration projects established to test certain principles of program organization or function. The former require an evaluation of the total package, while the latter would benefit more from a "variable-testing" design. We will return to this problem when we discuss the administrative considerations in evaluative research.

Another way of describing this difference in generality versus specificity between nonevaluative and evaluative research is to consider the *time and place* orientation of both of these forms of research. Evaluative research is largely limited to a certain time and place; nonevaluative research has as its goal as much "timelessness" or "spacelessness" as possible. The problem-solving objective of evaluative research places a premium upon administrative decision-making for some immediate need; hypothesis-testing in nonevaluative research seeks a generality which transcends the immediate phenomenon under investigation with as broad a generality in theory as is justified by the data. The more "controls" that an evaluative study can specify and the more specific it can make the various contingencies of success, the more useful it will be; the fewer "controls" or contingencies that have to be attached to a nonevaluative hypotheses the greater will be its theoretical value. "Too general" (that is, not directly applicable to the specific program in time and place) is an accusation often made by program directors of evaluative research; "too specific" (bound by particularly current time and space conditions) constitutes a frequent criticism by the theorist of the empirical scientist. Thus, in evaluative research we usually think of one-shot studies, while in nonevaluative research we stress continuity and cumulativeness of findings.

The inherent difference between evaluation studies as an aspect of applied research and nonevaluative or basic research is further reflected in the form taken by the statement of the problem. Essential to basic research is the formulation of a nonevaluative hypothesis relating two variables in a "the more 'a,' the more 'b' " format.[11] The object of the basic research study is to verify the existence of this relationship. There is no implication about the desirability or undesirability of "b" or about the possibility of manipulating "a." In evaluative research, on the other hand, the effect "b" becomes the valued or desired goal of some program "a" which is deliberately designed to change "b." Whereas "pure" science asks the question, "Is it a fact that 'a' is related to 'b'?" and then proceeds to test the "truth" of this relationship by means of experimental or field designs which attempt to hold other possible "causes" constant, "applied" science asks, "Does 'a' work effectively to change 'b'?" and attempts to answer this question empirically by setting up a program which manipulates "a" and then measuring the effect on "b." In the case of basic research, crucial significance is attached to an analysis of the process whereby "a" relates to "b" (intervening variable analysis), while in the case of applied research, it becomes relatively unimportant to understand why "a" produced "b."[12] This is largely what is meant when one characterizes basic research as being focused upon increased understanding, while applied research is more likely to be aimed at effective action.

We may illustrate this distinction with the following example. Epidemiological research (nonevaluative) was able to test the hypothesis that smoking ("a") was related to the occurrence of lung cancer ("b"). It was able to test this relationship by means of an intervening variable analysis which controlled on other possible causes related to both smoking and lung cancer (rural-urban residence, occupation, sex, age). Laboratory research (nonevaluative) helped to support this observed statistical correlation by providing data on the physiological process whereby nicotine from cigarettes could produce cancerous body tissue. In both cases of epidemiological and laboratory research, the objective was the discovery and explanation of the relationship between "a" and "b."

Based on such knowledge as the above, public health programs are being designed to reduce "b" by changing "a." Anti-smoking educational campaigns, smokers' clinics, legal restrictions, and the like are proposed to motivate, help, or restrict the behavior of the smoking public. Demonstration programs (evaluative) are being tested for their effectiveness in getting people to stop smoking. The immediate criterion by which the effectiveness of such programs will be judged is whether smokers stop smoking or nonsmokers do not begin to smoke. How and why such programs work or do not work is of tangential interest. The "pay-off" will be changed smoking habits. Whether or not such action reduces the incidence of lung cancer, while obviously crucial as an ultimate goal, is usually not a relevant criterion for an evaluation of the success of these particular health programs.

A relevant distinction is made by Radcliffe-Brown between *abstract* science (mathematics, logic), *pure natural* science (physiology, biology),

applied science (medicine, engineering), and *art* (medical practice).[13]
According to this classification, public health practice would be an art
based upon the applied science of medicine, which, in turn, draws upon
the pure sciences of physiology and biology utilizing the abstract sciences
of mathematics and logic. Given this interrelationship of science and
practice, it would seem that the two are not so much opposed to each
other as they are supplementary. Lewis describes this relationship as one
in which knowledge, action, and evaluation are essentially connected.[14]

There is obviously a strong link between "basic" and "applied" research,
with each feeding into the other. Increased understanding as a result of
basic research supplies the essential rationale for the design of applied
programs, while the evaluation of an applied program offers a valuable
test of the validity of the propositions offered by the basic research. Hovland stresses the importance of evaluative research as a fruitful source of
hypotheses for basic research.[15]

Another interesting aspect of evaluative research concerns its use in the
pursuit of basic research. Let us take methodological research as an example. Such fundamental concepts in pure research as reliability and validity are basically evaluative by nature. The determination of the reliability or validity of a research instrument asks the question, "Does it
work?" and the use of the instrument in the conduct of research becomes
applied or programmatic. This has been recognized by many methodologists who have pointed out the meaninglessness of measures of validity
not accompanied by the query, "Validity for what?"[16] It is made explicit in
the following statement by the U.S. National Health Survey, "The primary
purposes of the methodological studies are to appraise the effectiveness
and efficiency with which various aspects of the Survey program are
meeting their objectives."[17] In a similar sense, scientific theory may also be
evaluated in terms of its utility for ordering data or facts, while a pure research project as an administrative activity is itself subject to program
evaluation.

A distinction between evaluative and nonevaluative research which is
often made, but which we think is overly exaggerated, deals with the
greater personal involvement of the applied researcher in the outcome of
his project. Whereas negative results to a pure researcher may in themselves be a contribution to knowledge, a negative evaluation may well
mean the end of the program being studied. This possibility is especially
crucial, of course, for self-evaluation studies. It is argued, therefore, that
the value-laden nature of evaluation research interferes with scientific

objectivity. While this is undoubtedly true to a certain degree, it fails to take into account the possibility of intense personal commitment to a particular hypothesis on the part of the basic researcher and raises a question of psychological motivation or social roles rather than one of inherent objectivity or subjectivity. As Kaplan argues, "Whatever problems a scientist selects, he selects for a reason, and these reasons can be expected to relate to his values, or to the values of those who in one way or another influence his choice. This obvious point is often obscured, I think, by a too facile distinction between so-called 'pure' and 'applied' science, as though values are involved only in the latter. . . . The fact that a scientist has reasons for his choice of problems other than a thirst for knowledge or a love of truth scarcely implies that his inquiry will be biased thereby."[18]

One needs to recognize that, to a large extent, the procedures of scientific inquiry in themselves represent norms or values that govern the behavior of research workers. As Sjoberg points out, "Science is, after all, a social enterprise par excellence . . . his (the scientist's) actions are a product not merely of his socialization into the normative order of science but also of his involvement in the society that supports his scientific activity."[19] These norms serve as the criteria for evaluating the conduct of the researcher and are subject to social conventions regarding acceptable compromises from the ideal of scientific methodology. Such compromises represent realistic appraisals of available resources, accessibility of cases, cost, time, and the many other administrative considerations of even the "purest" research project. The question, it seems to us, is not one of "good" versus "evil" but of adhering as closely as is practical to the ideal rules of scientific inquiry, making certain to specify and justify where and when these rules have had to be adapted to reality.

METHODOLOGICAL APPROACHES TO EVALUATION

The scientific method is not bound by either subject matter or objective. Hence, evaluative research has no special methodology of its own. As "research" it adheres to the basic logic and rules of scientific method as closely as possible. Its canons of "proof" and its laws of inference are the same as those of any research project. It utilizes all available techniques for the collection and analysis of data and employs a wide variety of research designs. It may be carried out under experimental laboratory conditions or in the natural community. In other words, evaluative research is still research and it differs from nonevaluative research more in objective or purpose than in design or execution.

This position is taken quite explicitly by Klineberg who maintains. "The term evaluation should as far as possible be restricted to a process which satisfies such scientific criteria—objective, systematic, comprehensive. As such, it should be distinguished from all forms of assessment which take the form of one man's judgment of the success or failure of a project, no matter how sensible and wise that judgment appears to be. . . ."[20]

However, it must also be recognized that while all research has an underlying communality of logic and operations, each area of research, and often each project, reflects an adaptation of research design and techniques to the particular subject matter and research conditions of the special field or problem under investigation. Thus, for example, the natural sciences differ quite radically from the social sciences in their adaptation of the scientific method, and, even within each field, the disciplines of physics and geology or psychology and anthropology vary widely in research design and methodological techniques.

It is only natural, therefore, that many of the new developments in evaluation studies represent innovations dependent upon and borrowed from the current state of methodologist knowledge in the social science field. The question, as we see it, is not "Is evaluative research scientific?" so much as "How may evaluative research make the best use of available research designs and techniques?" A great deal of confusion and acrimonious debate exists in the field of evaluative research today because of the failure to recognize that scientific adequacy is a matter of degree and that decisions about the rigorousness of an evaluation study must represent a compromise between scientific requirements and administrative needs and resources.

While such compromises really exist to some degree even in the "purest" of basic research projects, they are almost endemic in evaluative research. The crucial question is "how much" compromise is permissible or desirable. An added complication, but really irrelevant to the basic argument, is the fact that a great deal of evaluative research is carried out by people who are not trained in research methods and are not equipped to make an informed decision about where and what compromises can be made. This point will also be discussed in more detail in the chapter on administrative considerations in evaluative research.

Perhaps the most productive answer to this controversy of "scientific" versus "nonscientific" evaluation lies in the recognition that, as Southard points out, an activity may be evaluated on the basis of one or more levels or types of measurement based on different value systems.[21] At the first level, we have the evaluation which a recipient group places on an activity according to its own personal objectives and value system. This represents the individual or group's estimate of the success or failure of a program in which he is taking part. At the second level, the evaluation represents the appraised worth of an activity as given by a group of "experts" or informed appraisers, usually on the basis of reasonable examination and comparison with other services. At the third level, we come to the scientific measurement of effectiveness made in terms of acceptable standardized procedures. This approach attempts to adhere as closely as possible to the rules of scientific methodology in setting up the evaluative research design and in utilizing evaluative instruments of determined reliability and validity.

Each of these levels presents somewhat different problems of research design and procedures. It is beyond the scope of the present volume to go into these problems in detail. This would require almost a separate text on methodology and, indeed, would duplicate much of what is to be found in any text on research methods. In this presentation we will concentrate on two major problems in methodology; first, the statement of objectives for an evaluative research project, and, second, considerations in the design of such a project. In both instances we will emphasize those adaptations of standard procedure with particular relevance for evaluative research.

FORMULATING THE EVALUATIVE RESEARCH PROBLEM

Research begins with a hypothesis: in nonevaluative research this hypothesis usually concerns the statement of a relationship between two variables, one of which is considered the independent or "causal" variable, while the other is viewed as the dependent or "effect" variable. The research project then proceeds, first, to verify the existence of this relationship by testing for possible spuriousness of causation (that is, where the dependent variable is related to the independent variable only because they both have some other factor in common) and, second, if the relationship is verified as a "true" one, to elaborate the conditions under which, and the process whereby, the independent variable affects the dependent variable. In general, we may speak of the first procedure as "descriptive," while the second may be called "explanatory."[22]

    In the same way, evaluative research also begins with the statement of a "causal" relationship hypothesized between some program or activity (the independent variable) and some desired effect (the dependent variable). The verification of this evaluative hypothesis requires the design of a research project which would show that the desired effect was more likely to occur in the presence of the program being evaluated than in its absence. Adopting the aforementioned terminology, we might label this a *descriptive evaluation*. Should one now wish to ask the further questions—"How do we know that the effect produced was really due to the program or activity?" and "Why or how did the program succeed in producing this effect?"—one would move into the more elaborate design of an *explanatory evaluation*.

    Before pointing out the implications of this distinction between descriptive and explanatory evaluation for the statement of objectives and the formulation of research design, let us examine briefly the underlying rationale of this approach. We conceive of a "causal" sequence in which our program becomes only one of many possible actions or events which may bring about (or deter) the desired effect. Furthermore, our program will not only influence the occurrence of the desired effect, but will have other effects as well. These conditions are often discussed in terms of "the multiplicity of causes" and "the interdependence of events" and may be diagrammed as follows:

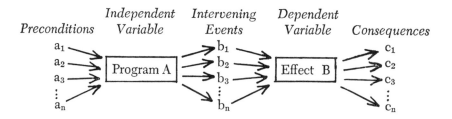

    No event has a single cause and each event has multiple effects. All events are interrelated in a complex causal nexus open by nature and subject to rational intervention. No single factor is a necessary and sufficient cause of any other factor, and change in one part of the system may occur without necessitating a completely new equilibrium.

    It should be recognized that acceptance of this open-system, naturalistic, multi-causal model as opposed to the closed-system, mechanistic, single-cause model has tremendous implication for the formulation of evaluative research projects. Evaluations of success must be made in terms of conditional probabilities involving attacks upon causal factors which are only disposing, contributory, or precipitating rather than determining. The effect of any single factor will depend upon other circumstances also being present and will itself reflect a host of antecedent events. These surrounding circumstances become an essential part of the "explanation" of the success or failure of attempts to influence any particular causal factor and combine to increase or decrease the probability but not the certainty of effective action. As Cornfield points out in relation to disease-causation, "the long and complicated chain between exposure to an agent and the subsequent development of the disease compels the consideration of probabilities and not certainties. The appropriate question to ask about agents in such situations is whether they alter the probability of an event's occurrence, and not whether they do or do not cause it."[23] This same line of reasoning would apply to prevention programs. Predictions of success or program objectives to be evaluated need to be stated in terms of conditions and probabilities; for example, "Given conditions A, B, and C, the proposal program has a .6 probability of attaining the desired goal (also stated in terms of some level of achievement and not total success)."

Lilienfeld approaches this problem of causality for medical and public health research in terms of necessary and sufficient causation. He states, "In medicine and public health it seems reasonable to adopt a pragmatic concept of causality . . . a factor may be defined as a cause of a disease, if the incidence of the disease is diminished when exposure to this factor is likewise diminished. . . . In biological phenomena, both these requirements (evidence that a factor is both a necessary and a sufficient condition for a disease) do not have to be met because of the existence of multiple causative factors. . . . Other additional factors included under the term 'susceptibility' are important."[24]

This approach to social causation has tremendous implications for prevention and intervention, and hence for program evaluation. It means, for one thing, that public service or social action programs must be evaluated within the context of other programs or events which may also affect the desired objective—either in a cumulative or cancelable way. It means that one must look at the preconditions or factors which influence the type of program activity that may be initiated and the intervening events that may include other effects than the desired one, some of which may be negative by nature. It also means that the desired effect must itself be examined for its own consequences, both short and long-term, desirable and undesirable.

These implications of a multi-causal approach for evaluation are recognized by a subcommittee of the National Advisory Mental Health Council for the planning of evaluation studies in the field of mental health, which concludes, "The concept of etiology as embraced by modern psychiatry differs from the simple cause and effect system of traditional medicine. It subscribes to a 'field theory' hypothesis in which the interactions and transactions of multiple factors eventuate in degrees of health or sickness. . . . Where and how to give weight to the interacting forces producing change where it is most relevant constitute the major problem in psychiatric etiology in the testing of this hypothesis. Until this problem is solved, the evaluation of mental health activities will remain difficult. At any rate this problem must be considered in any evaluation process."[25]

The statement of an evaluative hypothesis, we conclude, is almost as closely tied to an understanding of "causal" theories as is a nonevaluative hypothesis. While this condition is accepted as the *sine qua non* of basic research, it is often overlooked by the evaluative researcher who may tend to forget that a test of "Does it work?" presupposes some theory as to why one might expect it to work. An awareness of this fact would do much to reduce the large number of program evaluations which lack any clear-cut rationale for hypothesizing that program A will produce effect B, and perhaps, thereby, result in a greater number of "successful" evaluations.

Hyman points out that evaluative hypotheses are more likely to be concerned with specifying the conditions under which a given program will be more or less effective than with interpreting why this should be so. He suggests that this lack of concern with interpretation stems from an emphasis upon the success of the end product regardless of the reason. Positive results are usually accepted without question. Only negative results seem to require some explanation and this is usually by way of rationalizing the failure rather than understanding and accepting it.[26]

A strong position for explanation is taken by Bloch, who maintains that "the ultimate task of evaluative research is to demonstrate a lawful and understandable relation between change variables and treatment variables, not only a statistical relation."[27] This demonstration would require: (1) the definition and measurement of what is to be changed; (2) the specification of the active elements of the program designed to produce change; and (3) the relating of the change to the program elements in such a way as to justify the conclusion of a causal connection between the two.

One of the most significant implications of this approach to the statement of evaluative hypotheses involves the challenge not only to demonstrate that effect B follows program A, but also to "prove" that effect B was really due to program A. Some administrators may argue that so long as B occurs it does not really matter whether A was the actual cause. This will be legitimate insofar as A is not a spurious cause of B. However, if A is spurious, one may institute an expensive, broad program based on A only to find (or, even worse, not to find because the evaluation is not continuous) that the desired effect no longer occurs because of a change in the "true" cause which may have been only momentarily related to A.

To achieve this test of "spuriousness," the evaluative project must include an analysis of the intervening process between program and result. In evaluative as opposed to nonevaluative research, however, the manipulatability of these intervening variables rather than their explanatory power is more likely to influence their selection. As Hyman points out, "In the evaluative inquiry, the range of attempts of explanation is also usually fairly well-defined in advance and limited in number, although somewhat wider than in the theoretical inquiry. . . . The evaluative inquiry often deals not with refined and unitary variables and their intrinsic effects but with manipulable constellations or compounds of unitary variables, for example, with programs."[28]

Perhaps the classic example of an evaluation study which demonstrated the importance of including intervening variables in the formulation of the evaluative hypothesis is that of the so-called "Hawthorne Effect." Roethlisberger and Dickson in an evaluation of a program designed to increase worker productivity found that the specific program activities such as changes in illumination, rest periods, and hours of work were "spuriously" effective, since productivity tended to increase no matter what change was made. They concluded that the "true" cause was the intervening variable of interest and concern on the part of management.[29] This same logic underlies the standard clinical evaluation design of a "blind" and "double-blind" test, involving the use of a "placebo" to control the intervening variable of personal influence and suggestibility. We will return to this problem when we discuss the conceptual and methodological problems in defining the independent or causal variables in evaluative research.

An awareness of the importance of a multiple-factor approach to evaluation including the need to be sensitive to the intervening process probably underlies the constant emphasis given by the literature to "built-in" evaluative research. This approach stresses the dynamic nature of most action and service programs and argues for an evaluative research design which becomes an inherent part of the service program itself. Built-in or ongoing evaluation recognizes that there are many changing conditions which govern the operation of a program, partly because of forces beyond the control of the program administrator, but also partly because of a "feedback" of information from the evaluation itself which may affect both objectives and procedures. To provide for this form of continuous evaluation, one must formulate the evaluative research hypotheses in terms of contingencies and developments that may occur during the course of the program and that may require the collection of new or additional data. Thus, for example, a built-in evaluation design in a mass tuberculosis x-ray campaign in New York City indicated that the assumed informal community organization was almost totally lacking in the slum neighborhoods being studied and required a shift in both objectives and procedures from a stress on utilizing existing community forces to mobilizing a largely disorganized community.[30] To continue the evaluation study on the basis of the original hypothesis would have been tantamount to evaluating a nonexistent stimulus.

We next turn our attention to the formulation of the research design for evaluative research. Too often, the collection of data for evaluative purposes proceeds without sufficient attention to the feasibility and appropriateness of the method used. Research design for evaluation, as we shall see in the next chapter, presents problems similar to those of research design in general.

N O T E S   T O   C H A P T E R   V

1. *Planning Evaluations of Mental Health Programs.* Report of the Second Meeting of the Advisory Council on Mental Health Demonstrations, Milbank Memorial Fund, New York, 1958, p. 14.
2. Dyar, Robert, "General Summary of Conference on Research Methodology and Potential in Community Health and Preventive Medicine," *Annals of the New York Academy of Sciences,* vol. 107, May 22, 1963, p. 805.
3. *Ibid.,* p. 807.
4. See, for example, Gouldner, Alvin W., "Theoretical Requirements of the Applied Social Sciences, "*American Sociological Review,* vol. 22, February, 1957, pp. 92–102. We may conceive of this continuum as follows: Pure research aimed at accumulation of knowledge → Basic re-

search with relevance for application → Action research aimed at the process of application → Engineering research dealing with the actual conditions of application → Evaluative research focused upon administrative decisions following application.

5. Fleck, Andrew C., "Evaluation Research Programs in Public Health Practice," *Annals of the New York Academy of Sciences,* vol. 107, May 22, 1963, p. 717.

6. Thus, evaluation "has characteristics that distinguish it from that type of research whose objective is the accumulation and analysis of data in order to formulate hypothesis and theory for the sake of new knowledge itself, irrespective of judgment of the value of the knowledge." The Subcommittee on Evaluation of Mental Health Activities, Community Science Committee, National Advisory Mental Health Council, *A Review of the Problem of Evaluating Mental Health Activities.* National Institute of Mental Health, Bethesda, Md., 1954.

7. Merton, Robert K., "The Role of Applied Social Science in the Formation of Policy," *Philosophy of Science,* vol. 16, July, 1949, p. 176.

8. Hyman, Herbert, *Survey Design and Analysis.* The Free Press, Glencoe, Ill., 1955, p. 312.

9. Zetterberg, Hans L., *On Theory and Verification in Sociology.* The Bedminster Press, Totowa, N.J., 1963, pp. 5–10.

10. Hovland, Carl I., Arthur A. Lumsdaine, and Fred D. Sheffield, *Experiments in Mass Communication.* Princeton University Press, Princeton, N.J., 1949.

11. A good discussion on the nature of hypothesis formulation and testing may be found in Nagel, Ernest, *The Structure of Science,* Harcourt, Brace and Co., 1961; and Churchman, C. West, *Theory of Experimental Inference,* Macmillan Co., New York, 1948.

12. An excellent presentation of intervening variable analysis may be found in Lazarsfeld, Paul F., and Morris Rosenberg, editors, *The Language of Social Research,* The Free Press, Glencoe, Ill., 1955.

13. Radcliffe-Brown, A. R., *A Natural Science of Society.* The Free Press, Glencoe, Ill., 1957, pp. 8–11.

14. Lewis, C. I., "An Analysis of Knowledge and Valuation," The Paul Carus Foundation Lectures VII. The Open Court Publishing Co., La Salle, Ill., 1946, p. 3.

15. Hovland, Carl I., and others, *op. cit.,* pp. 258–259.

16. Jenkins, John G., "Validity for What?" *Journal of Consulting Psychology,* vol. 10, 1946, pp. 93–98.

17. *Origin, Program and Operations of the U.S. National Health Survey.* National Center for Health Statistics, Washington, Series I, No. 1, August, 1963, p. 14.

18. Kaplan, Abraham, *The Conduct of Inquiry.* Chandler Publishing Co., San Francisco, 1964, pp. 381–382.

19. Sjoberg, Gideon, "Research Methodology: A Sociology of Knowledge Perspective." Paper prepared for presentation to the Sociological Research Association, Chicago, August 31, 1965, pp. 1–2.

20. Klineberg, Otto, "The Problem of Evaluation," *International Social Science Bulletin,* vol. 7, no. 3, 1955, p. 347.
21. Southard, Curtis G., *Symposium on the Evaluation of Community Mental Health Programs.* National Institute of Mental Health, 1952–1953, Seminar Series, November 25, 1952, as reported in *Evaluation in Mental Health.* Public Health Service, Publication No. 413, Government Printing Office, Washington, 1955, pp. 17–18.
22. A great deal has been written about this model for formulating and testing hypotheses and need not be elaborated here. See, for example, Hyman, Herbert, *op. cit.;* Zetterberg, Hans L., *op. cit.;* and Lazarsfeld, Paul F., and Morris Rosenberg, editors, *op. cit.*
23. Cornfield, Jerome, "Principles of Research," *American Journal of Mental Deficiency,* vol. 64, September, 1959, pp. 242–252. It is important not to confuse interrelatedness of factors with equality of effect. As Boran cautions, "Interrelatedness and reciprocity do not necessarily mean, however, that all factors are of the same weight, that there is no primacy, 'no place where the thread begins.' It is not unscientific to speak of a *basic* structure, if, in fact, there are some institutional areas which play a relatively determining and directing role in social change. Besides, it is inescapable in actual research and explanation of the facts collected to choose a starting-point." Boran, Behice, "Sociology in Retrospect," *American Journal of Sociology,* vol. 52, January, 1947, p. 320.
24. Lilienfeld, Abraham M., "Epidemiological Methods and Inferences in Studies of Noninfectious Diseases," *Public Health Reports,* vol. 72, January, 1957, p. 56.
25. *Evaluation in Mental Health, op. cit.,* p. 11.
26. Hyman, Herbert, *op. cit.,* pp. 315–316.
27. Bloch, Donald A., "Measuring Change in the Mental Health Status of Children." Paper prepared for presentation at the 1964 Annual Meetings of the American Orthopsychiatric Association, Chicago.
28. Hyman, Herbert, *op. cit.,* pp. 312–314.
29. Roethlisberger, F.J., and W.J. Dickson, *Management and the Worker.* Harvard University Press, Cambridge, Mass., 1939.
30. Metzner, Charles A., and Gerald Gurin, *Personal Response and Social Organization in a Health Campaign.* University of Michigan, Bureau of Public Health Economics, Research Series No. 9, Ann Arbor, 1960.

CHAPTER VI

The Evaluative Research Design

In the research process, the statement of the problem including the formulation of hypotheses is followed by the laying out of a study design for the collection and analysis of data bearing upon these hypotheses. This design indicates the general approach to be used, for example, experimental, field survey, clinical observation, and specifies the actual procedures for selecting the population to be studied, for administering the research instruments or tests, for determining the reliability and validity of the measurements made, and for analyzing the data so as to accept, reject, or qualify the hypotheses being studied.

This process applies to all forms of research, evaluative research included. However, the extent to which a research worker adheres to all of the basic requirements of this process represents, by and large, a compromise between the level of incontrovertible proof desired and the administrative resources at hand. As we have stated elsewhere,

1. It seems to us futile to argue whether a certain design is "scientific." The design is the plan of study and, as such, is present in all studies. It is not a case of scientific or not scientific, but rather one of good or less good design.
2. The proof of hypotheses is never definitive. The best one can hope to do is to make more or less plausible a series of alternative hypotheses.
3. There is no such thing as a single "correct" design. . . . Hypotheses can be studied by different methods using different designs.
4. All research design represents a compromise dictated by the many practical considerations that go into social research.
5. A research design is not a highly specific plan to be followed without deviation, but rather a series of guideposts to keep one headed in the right direction.[1]

Nowhere are these considerations more applicable than to evaluative research, with its strong emphasis upon administrative decision-making rather than the acquisition of knowledge. But before one can compromise intelligently one must be aware of basic principles. These principles of research design and of measurement constitute the subject matter of texts on methodology. Since they are so basic to the design of an evaluative re-

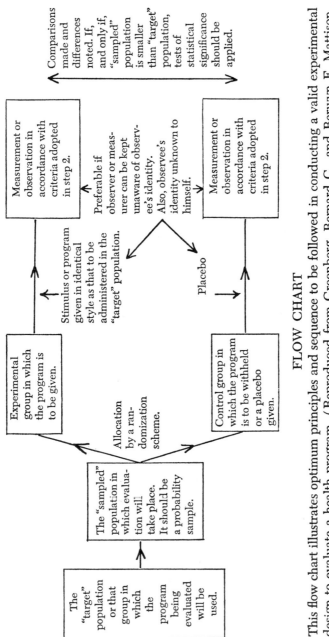

FLOW CHART

This flow chart illustrates optimum principles and sequence to be followed in conducting a valid experimental design to evaluate a health program. (Reproduced from Greenberg, Bernard G., and Berwyn F. Mattison, "The Whys and Wherefores of Program Evaluation," *Canadian Journal of Public Health*, vol. 46, July, 1955, p. 298.)

search project, we will briefly summarize some of the more relevant considerations.[2]

The application of the research model to evaluative research is clearly presented by Greenberg and Mattison in terms of a graphic flow chart involving the definition of a target population, the drawing of a representative sample for study, the allocation of this sample at random into experimental and control groups, the administration of the program to one group and a placebo to the other, and the comparison of resulting differences between the two groups. This model, it is recognized, is "an optional one . . . deviations and compromises will have to be made."[3] (See Flow Chart.)

This model represents the ideal experimental design from which *all* adaptations must be derived. No matter what approach one uses or what concessions one is forced to make because of operational limitations, the basic logic of proof and verification will be traceable to this model. It is important to remember that there is not one but a set of experimental designs, and that there is no one best way to design all evaluative studies.

VARIATIONS IN EVALUATIVE RESEARCH DESIGN

Campbell offers the following classification of experimental designs, where X represents the exposure of a group to the experimental variable or event (the public service or social action program in the present instance), and O refers to the process of observation or measurement (of the desired effect). Furthermore, X's and O's in a given row refer to the same specific persons, while parallel rows represent equivalent or matched samples of persons. Temporal order is indicated by the left-to-right dimension.[4]

1. *The One-Shot Case Study*

X O

Observations or measurements are made of the individual or group only after exposure to the program being evaluated. This is probably the weakest and yet the most common evaluative research design. There is no baseline measurement of the study group with which to compare the post-program measure and no control group which has not been exposed to the program to assure that the observed effect was due to the experimental stimulus or program. Quite frequently in public service research this design gives rise to testimonial evidence in favor of a program. Individuals who participate in the program testify as to its effectiveness on the basis of personal experience. This is largely what happens in various "faith" cures and, to some extent, forms the basis for many evaluations of psychotherapeutic programs. While this design can reassure the program administrator that his activities are being well received by his clients, it really provides little evidence as to its actual effectiveness.

It is possible to bolster the plausibility of evidence secured by means of this "after only" design by certain checks upon the validity of the individual's testimony. An attempt can be made retrospectively to reproduce the individual's situation before exposure. While obviously subject to a memory and halo bias, at least some data may be secured to serve as a substitute "before" measure. By subdividing the subjects according to differential amount and types of exposure to the program one may be able to show that increased exposure produced a greater effect. While helpful in some cases, this type of measurement is subject to a self-selective sampling bias in that those individuals most susceptible to an effect or most favorable to the program are likely to expose themselves to a greater degree.

2. *The One-Group, Pre-test, Post-test Design*

$$O_1 X O_2$$

In this evaluative design, the researcher introduces a base measure before the program is put into effect, to be followed by an "after" measure at the conclusion of the program. While this design does permit one to measure change objectively, it does not allow one to attribute this change to the program being evaluated. Five main sources of "error" are still possible: (1) other extraneous events may occur simultaneously as the experimental stimulus which influence the effect being measured; (2) the effect may be due to "unstimulated" change as a result of time alone, that is, some people improve with or without exposure to the program; (3) the "before" measure itself may constitute a stimulus to change regardless of the program itself; (4) the "after" measure may reflect time changes in measurement due to fatigue or instrument unreliability; and (5) unreliability may produce statistical regression with shifting values toward the mean.

3. *The Static Group Comparison*

$$X O_1$$
$$O_2$$

Two groups are compared in this approach, one having been exposed to the program and the other not. If the exposed group shows a significantly higher incidence of the desired condition or behavior, it is assumed to be attributable to the program. This is really the basic logic of much epidemiological research. Two groups with varying frequency of a disease condition are compared and differences between the two are viewed as possible causes of the disease. However, this design affords no way of knowing that the two groups were equivalent *before* the program, although selective matching and retrospective measures of the two groups according to pre-program characteristics may help.

4. *Pre-test, Post-test, Control Group Design*

$$O_1 \; X \; O_2$$
$$O_3 \quad O_4$$

We finally come to the classic experimental design as presented previously in the flow chart of evaluative research. We begin by setting up two equivalent groups which are as alike as possible before the program is put into effect. Such equivalence is best obtained by random assignment to experimental and control groups. Where this is not administratively feasible, one may have to resort to selective matching. Then, a "before" measure is made to determine the base line from which change is to be evaluated, and for providing a check on the equivalence of the two groups. One of the groups (the experimental group) is exposed to the program being evaluated while the other (the control group) is not, care being taken to keep the groups from coming into contact with each other. At the conclusion of the program (or at appropriate time intervals), an "after" measure is made which may be compared with the "before" measure for both experimental and control groups to indicate the changes produced by the experimental program.

This design is so crucial we repeat it in another form;[5]

	Before	After	
Experimental	X_1	X_2	$d = X_2 - X_1$
Control	X^1_1	X^1_2	$d^1 = X^1_2 - X^1_1$

The test of program effectiveness is indicated by the significance of the difference between d and d^1.

The logic of this design is foolproof. Ideally, there is no element of fallibility. Whatever differences are observed between the experimental

and control groups, once the above conditions are satisfied, must be attributable to the program being evaluated. One source of possible contamination exists if the process of making the "before" and "after" measures
can conceivably interact with the experimental variable.[6] For example,
the mere act of making the "before" measure may sensitize the experimental group to the program that is to follow. Solomon suggests the
following extension of the basic experimental design in such cases;[7]

5. *The Solomon Four-Group Design*

$$O_1 \; X \; O_2$$
$$O_3 \quad O_4$$
$$X \, O_5$$
$$O^6$$

This design controls and measures both the experimental effect and the
possible interaction effects of the measuring process itself. Where such interaction effects are highly important and one is not in a position to set up
a four-group design, it is probably better to use a modified static group
comparison (No. 3) in which equivalent experimental and control groups
are selected before the evaluation; the program is administered to the experimental group only but no measurements are made of either group until after the program is completed.

THE "PLACEBO" EFFECT

A related interactional effect of the evaluative process itself which might
interfere with a measurement of effectiveness concerns the influence of
suggestion upon both subjects and evaluators. While this problem has not
been adequately discussed in the general literature on program evaluation,
it has become standard procedure in clinical and drug evaluation studies.
It is well recognized in clinical research that knowledge on the part of
either the patient or the doctor that a drug or therapy is being administered may influence the results of the evaluation. For this reason, the control group is often given a placebo or an inert substance resembling the
active drug but lacking the hypothesized effective agent. In a "blind" test,
the subject does not know whether he is receiving the active drug being
evaluated or the inactive placebo. In a "double-blind," neither the subject
nor the experimenter is aware of which is the drug and which is the
placebo.

A great deal has been written about this evaluative research design and
we need only summarize the main features here.

Briefly, it is a control device to prevent bias from influencing results. On the one hand, it rules out the effects of the hopes and anxieties of the patient by giving both the drug under investigation and a placebo of identical appearance in such a way that the subject (the first "blind" man) does not know which he is receiving. On the other hand, it also rules out the influence of preconceived hopes of, and unconscious communication by, the investigator or observer by keeping him (the second "blind" man) ignorant of whether he is prescribing a placebo or an active drug. At the same time, the technique provides another control, a means of comparison with the magnitude of placebo effects.[8]

In essence, the use of a placebo in a double-blind evaluative research design provides a means of separating the intrinsic effects of the stimulus from the extraneous effects of the *act* of administering the stimulus. In the case of medical treatment, one may attribute the effectiveness of the placebo to the symbolic power of the physician and the drug, to the motivation of, or social pressure upon, the patient to respond to the treatment,[9] or to belief on the part of the physician himself in the effectiveness of his therapy.[10] Before the growth of modern, scientific medicine, a major proportion of "cures" produced by witch-doctors and primitive medicine men were undoubtedly largely the result of the placebo effect. As described by Shapiro, "the history of medical treatment until relatively recently is the history of the placebo effect."[11] Frank points out that, "Until the last few decades most medications prescribed by physicians were pharmacologically inert. That is, physicians were prescribing placebos without knowing it."[12] Today, this is still the probable basis for the so-called "faith" cures reported by almost all known religious or mystical sects—and non-Western medicine in general.

The crucial question for the present analysis of evaluative designs in public service research is, "To what extent may the effectiveness of public service programs be due to 'faith' or the symbolic power of official agencies rather than the intrinsic components of the program?" And, if we have reason to believe this can occur, is it possible to design evaluation studies of public service programs involving the use of "dummy" programs and double-blind administration techniques?

Our analysis of the first question leads us to conclude that there probably are a great many public service and social action programs that "work" largely because both the public and the practitioner have faith in them. James points out that, "During a polio outbreak of 15 years ago some health workers were severely criticized for not closing schools and swimming pools, while others who took these epidemiologically unproved steps received high praise. Perhaps the real objective involved was fear and insecurity which is satisfied by forthright expert action, no matter how unproved its effectiveness."[13]

Undoubtedly, many public service programs are effective not because of the specific program activities undertaken, but rather through suggestion and authority which produce security and confidence in the individual and the community. As in the case of the "Hawthorne Effect," it may not matter what changes are made so long as the public feels someone is looking out for its welfare. Webster's Dictionary defines a placebo as, "a medicine, especially an inactive one, given merely to satisfy a patient."[14] How many public service programs are carried out primarily to "satisfy" the public in the absence of any convincing evidence of their inherent effectiveness?

From a conceptual point of view, the basic question is the extent to which the placebo represents a "spurious" rather than a "true" cause of some desired effect. If a person's health improves as a result of the "act" of being treated, instead of the medication or treatment per se, what makes the "act" spurious? One may hypothesize a causal sequence in which the subjective factor of "faith" or "suggestibility" becomes an intervening variable between the act of providing treatment and the improvement of the health condition. We may diagram the "true" and "spurious" sequences as follows:

True: Drug A   →   Physiological   →   Reduction of Disease-
                      Changes   Causing Conditions

Spurious: Act of Giving   →   Belief in   →   Relief of
                 Drug A   Effectiveness   Symptoms

Perhaps the basic issue is whether the "cure" is true, for example, there is a change in disease state; or spurious, for example, the disease remains, but the symptoms are alleviated. If the latter, it is obvious that the sick individual experiencing a placebo effect may actually be in a more dangerous position because of a false sense of improvement which keeps him from seeking further medical care.

However, this is not always the case, since the placebo effect may actually result in a condition which is positive to the treatment of the illness, that is, the relief of anxiety which is detrimental to a mental illness or even a heart condition. We note, however, the reluctance of the medical practitioner to accept even the latter as "legitimate." For example, Reader and Goss state, ". . . the relationship between a particular drug and the patient's report that he has fewer attacks of angina while taking it may be completely misleading; he may simply feel more secure as a result of treatment and have fewer attacks."[15] Such a finding would be "spurious" in the evaluation of the pharmacological action of the drug, but is it "spurious" as an evaluation of the effectiveness of the therapy for reducing attacks of angina? An interesting question which goes beyond the purposes of the present discussion would be to ask why is a "cure" based on faith illegitimate while one due to the program itself is not? A serious problem for evaluative research in public service is the extent to which public service activities are based upon proven principles rather than unproven assumptions whose main legitimacy rests upon tradition and authority.

The application of a placebo, double-blind, evaluative research design to public service programs is largely hypothetical. We cannot readily set up placebo public service programs with all the trappings of the true program except for those specific activities which are supposed to make the program effective. Nor can we "hide" the nature of these two programs from both the community and the public service workers. We can only speculate, as we have done, on the implications of such a design for interpreting the effectiveness of many present-day public service programs.

One extension of the research designs presented above would help to determine the extent to which the effectiveness of a public health program was related to specific components of that program rather than to the existence of the program per se. This would involve the addition of alternate programs with varying combinations of specific components for comparative evaluation. Using the classic "pre-test, post-test, control group design" (No. 4 above), we might diagram this as follows:

$$O_1 \quad X_1 \quad O_2$$
$$O_3 \quad X_2 \quad O_4$$
$$O_5 \quad X_3 \quad O_6$$
$$O_7 \qquad\quad O_8$$

This design would be especially effective for evaluating program components if the variations, X_1, X_2, X_3, and so on consisted of programs that were alike in all respects except the particular component being evaluated. Quite elaborate experimental designs are available for evaluating various "treatments" according to different combinations of components.[16] The evaluation of alternative programs also provides a measure of the relative efficiency of different approaches. For example, an evaluation of health and sanitation programs in Egypt employed an experimental design which compared five villages according to different combinations of program components.[17] Meyer and Borgatta stress the value of comparative evaluative research designs for allocating priorities to limited funds and resources. They state, "Any single evaluative research should be placed in the perspective of comparisons between alternative approaches that might be available to deal with a problem. It is not sufficient to determine that an agency's program is better than neglect. An agency . . . must therefore justify its existence in terms of efficiency within a competitive economy of agencies."[18] Increasing demands for all forms of public service—police, education, welfare, housing—have forced public service into the political arena in a competition for limited community support and tax funds and evaluations of any single public service program will inevitably be measured against similar evaluations of other service programs.

THE LONGITUDINAL STUDY DESIGN

Another form of comparative evaluation involves a research design which permits one to compare the effectiveness of a program over a period of time. By making evaluations at different points in time, one may check on the progress of the program toward its objectives and, at the same time, use the earlier measurements of subjects as a form of self-control against subsequent measures. This will be similar to a clinical evaluation design in which the subject acts as his own control by studying him at different points in time in a series which both administers and withholds the drug or treatment being evaluated. We might diagram this evaluative design as follows:

$$O_1 \; X_1 \; O_2 \; - \; O_3 \; X_2 \; O_4 \; - \; O_5$$

While this design has obvious weaknesses in that previous exposures undoubtedly have carry-over effects on subsequent tests, it does provide a valuable model for ongoing or continuous evaluation studies.[19] This model is particularly appropriate where one is dealing with long-term, developmental programs rather than short-term, discrete programs. It permits the measurement of change and the feedback of information into the program, enabling one to take account of new conditions. Since most programs in public service and social action are designed to meet ongoing problems, this design is often more productive than the one-shot evaluative study.

Any single-shot evaluation study really constitutes a sample of one selected at a particular moment from an ongoing program. One must be able to make a reasonable assumption that the particular time at which the evaluation is made is "typical" and that the program itself is fairly stable and will not undergo constant revision. Some obvious factors to be considered are seasonal variations and time of day or day of week. A dynamic program would require a series of separate evaluations made at different times and perhaps under different conditions. Even a static program which is concerned with maintaining a certain fixed standard may require a continuous series of evaluations according to some time-sampling plan to achieve a form of "quality control."

A variation of this design would involve the use of different populations at different stages or cycles of the program. If these successive cohort groups were representative of the same target population, it would be possible to evaluate effectiveness at different points in time without the carry-over effect of the previous design. This design is obviously essential when the act of evaluation "destroys" or drastically changes the object being evaluated, as would be the case in many treatment programs. It is also a more efficient design when it becomes difficult or impossible to keep in contact with the original cohort. The following diagram would represent this type of evaluative design;

$$X_1 \quad O_1$$
$$X_2 \quad O_2$$
$$X_3 \quad O_3$$

This design will not, however, permit the analysis of internal changes in terms of the characteristics of those individuals who were changed as a result of the program. The analysis of such internal change constitutes, of course, the basic advantage of the so-called longitudinal or panel design in social and epidemiological research. This design has received a great deal of attention in the literature as a means of determining prediction variables for identifying high-risk groups and as a method for the study of causation.[20] The analytic power of this design also extends to evaluative research as a means of answering the question, "How do we know that the desired effect was the result of our program activities?"

The following diagram summarizes the six possible interrelationships between two variables measured at two points in time:[21]

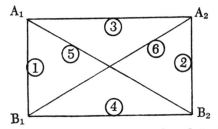

If A represents the program being evaluated and B the desired effect, then the crucial relationship concerns the change from B absent at time 1 to B present at time 2 following the introduction of A. This model may also be used to test for mutual effects when one has reason to believe that the desired effect may in reality be the cause rather than, or as well as, the effect of the exposure. This phenomenon occurs fairly frequently in education programs intended to increase information or interest where we find that the better informed or more interested individuals are more likely to expose themselves to the education program. We may say that A determines B when relationship No. 5 ($r_{A_1 B_2}$) exceeds relationship No. 6 ($r_{B_1 A_2}$), while B determines A when No. 6 exceeds No. 5. In other words, the effect should correlate higher with a prior "cause" than a subsequent "cause."

From this discussion of evaluative research designs, it should be apparent that evaluation studies present many of the same problems of isolating cause and measuring effect as any other type of research project. The ideal evaluation study would follow the classic experimental model, but, as is the case for most areas of research, evaluative research projects, by and large, utilize some variation or adaptation of this model.[22]

THE THREE MAIN CONDITIONS OF EVALUATIVE RESEARCH

In the remainder of this chapter, we will examine in more detail three main conditions of the experimental method as they apply to evaluative research: (1) sampling equivalent experimental and control groups; (2) isolation and control of the stimulus; and (3) definition and measurement of criteria of effect.

1. *Sampling Equivalent Experimental and Control Groups.* The problems of selecting subjects for evaluative research projects may be discussed under three headings: (1) defining the target group or population universe for evaluation; (2) selecting the specific samples to be included in the study; and (3) dividing the sample into equivalent experi-

mental and control groups. In regard to the first problem, the definition of the target group will depend to a large degree upon how the results of the evaluation study are to be applied. Any sample is only a smaller representation of some larger whole. The crucial question is, "To which groups am I going to generalize the results of my evaluation?" As described by Cochran, "The people from whom data are obtained—the sample—are of interest only insofar as the data tell us something about some larger group of people whom statisticians call the population or universe. Further, results obtained from a sample can be extended to a larger population with logical soundness only if the sample is, in a certain technical sense, a probability sample drawn from that population."[23]

We have already noted that in the case of an evaluation of a demonstration program, it is important that the demonstration program approximate as closely as possible the full-scale operating programs which might be established as a result of the demonstration. The same principle applies to the definition of the group upon whom an evaluation study is based. If the results are to be meaningful, the group one uses in the evaluative project should be representative of the target group for the full-scale operating program.

It is obvious, for example, that conclusions based upon an evaluation study sample composed only of cooperative volunteers would have limited application to a larger population, many of whom may be apathetic or even antagonistic toward the program. And yet many evaluation studies continue to be conducted upon groups of people convenient to work with and willing to be studied. If one must choose this type of population for an evaluation study, it is essential that one at least know how it differs from the larger population at whom the program will ultimately be aimed.

The selection of a representative sample of appropriate size from the defined target population presents no unique problems for evaluative research. As is true for all research, representativeness must be governed by randomness of selection whether simple, systematic, or stratified.[24] The use of judgmental or "purposive" samples may be dictated by practical necessity, but, if used, it should be recognized that sampling errors and biases cannot be computed or controlled for such samples. The size of the sample to be selected will depend a great deal upon the anticipated degree of effect—the greater the degree, the smaller the sample required —and the amount of "breakdown" analysis desired—the more population subgroupings and the more variables introduced simultaneously, the larger the sample will have to be.

The third and most difficult requirement of sampling for evaluative research concerns the setting up of equivalent experimental and control groups. We have already noted the importance of having two such matched groups and, for the present, will concentrate on the administrative difficulty of obtaining such groups in the evaluation of ongoing service programs.

In the laboratory situation, we can meet this requirement quite simply by allocating our experimental animals at random to experimental and control groups. In public service programs and social research in general, we have no such freedom. In part, this represents the practical difficulty of establishing administrative procedures which permit random assignment into experimental or control groups or, in the case of community programs, of finding equivalent communities, and, in part, the ethical problem of withholding service from a group that needs it. As Blenkner points out, "No casework agency is so dedicated to science as to permit it to make a random sort of its applicants, offering help to one half, while merely following up the other half to see what happens to them."[25]

Even if such assignment were possible, the subjects who seek help or who take advantage of a program are self-selected and there is really no way of forcing the noncooperative person to join in an experiment. As Hyman and his colleagues indicate, "The evaluator rarely has control over the flow of subjects into a program. Selection is governed either by the subject himself when he is favorably disposed to a program, or by the agency which recruits in terms of the wish to have particular subjects and programs joined. In the latter instance, the subjects are regarded as especially appropriate for or predisposed to the program, and the program may consequently have a peculiar clientele."[26]

These authors suggest a possible solution through the use of alternative programs given to a variety of experimental groups. Thus, the ethical argument against denying treatment is met while, at the same time, one may also compare the relative effectiveness of different approaches. Another suggestion offered by these investigators is borrowed from an evaluation of psychotherapeutic programs in which the subjects who requested therapy were asked to postpone treatment for a period of sixty days, during which tests were made to determine how much spontaneous improvement occurred, with the group thereby becoming its "own-control."[27] A similar design was employed by Hyman and his colleagues in their own evaluation of the Encampment for Citizenship.

Borgatta discusses the many kinds of resistance to control groups in evaluative research by service agencies. He challenges their argument that withholding treatment means depriving clientele of services to which they are entitled. This condition he regards as the *sine qua non* of scientific evaluation research and feels that any agency which is unwilling to set up administrative procedures to permit such evaluation lacks a proper climate for judging whether their services are worth providing.[28] Meyer and Borgatta carried out one of the few really carefully designed and executed evaluation studies in the field of rehabilitation, but found that out of 116 potentially eligible subjects, only 32 qualified for the experiment, which permitted the assignment of only 16 cases each to experimental and control groups.[29] Truly, as Smith observed, "Practical difficulties of gaining access to genuinely comparable groups have made the use of this ideal design a rarity."[30]

Given the difficulty of matching by random assignment, social researchers have developed methods of matching experimental and control groups according to group characteristics and utilizing techniques for covariance analysis which permit controlled comparisons without actual matching. An excellent analysis by Mathen of the advantages and disadvantages of different methods of matching concludes that, in general, there is little gain by either internal (experimental allocation) or external (group characteristics) over covariance analyses in precision attained.[31] The advantages of matching (either internal or external) are the possibility of making a "pure" comparison (a comparison not involving adjustments based on arbitrary assumptions); its potentiality for reducing the bias associated with known attributes; and elegance in statistical analysis through paired comparisons. The disadvantages are the reduction to small sizes of the samples available for comparison; the difficulty arising in prospective studies due to sampling mortality; and limitations due to the discovery of new covariates after the study has begun. The advantages of an analysis of covariance are its ability to reduce bias; its flexibility in adjusting for new covariates as they are discovered; and its utilization of all the available information. The disadvantages of this form of analysis are its dependence upon an arbitrary mathematical model; large sampling errors when cell frequencies are small; and the complexity of the analysis when a large number of attributes are involved. There is little question that most evaluative research in public service and social action areas will have to depend upon covariance analysis to approximate the controlled conditions of the laboratory experiment.

2. *Isolation and Control of the Stimulus—The Independent Program Variable.* A second major methodological problem in evaluative research

concerns the formulation, isolation, and manipulation of the variable which is intended to produce the desired effects. It is obviously important that the program to be evaluated be as clearly defined as possible—or else one will never know *what* is being evaluated. We have already discussed some of the conceptual problems involved in specifying the program dimensions for evaluative purposes in a previous chapter; in this chapter we will limit our discussion to methodological problems in testing the adequacy of this specification of program variables. This test involves two major questions: *What* is producing the desired change? *Why* is this change coming about?

Methodologically, finding the answers to these two questions becomes a search for "causes." As we have indicated, in an area of multiplicity of causal factors and interdependence of cause and effect, such a search becomes largely one of testing for associations between some arbitrarily selected causes and the hypothesized effects. It is worth noting that this state of affairs is not limited to public service or social action programs, for, "The modern physicist thinks of a phenomenon he wants to understand as an event taking place in a field. . . . This field is a complex of forces and conditions which may be plotted by axes and coordinates. . . . The goal is not so much to find or manipulate a 'cause' as to discover a means of effective intervention."[32]

On an elementary level, this second condition of evaluative research requires that, at a minimum, the program being evaluated be described in as much detail as possible, with emphasis being given to those aspects of the program which are believed to be crucial to its effectiveness. These program components include not only the operating procedures, but also the type of staff carrying out the program and the environment or setting in which the program is being conducted.

Hyman points out that, "Our conclusions are sounder and our understanding is greater if we can distinguish whether it is formal program or the staff that is responsible for the outcome. It also becomes clear in the course of observation that specific personnel executing the same formal tasks vary greatly in their manner and in the quality of their performance."[33] As an example, he mentions several fairly elaborate evaluative research studies of college educational programs which emphasized the importance of *how* a program was carried out as well *what* the program encompassed.[34]

Two vital elements affecting the evaluation of demonstration projects are the nature of the professional identity and the social organization of the project. In a demonstration program, it is particularly important to separate the program itself as a stimulus to change from the staff and organization carrying out the program. Borgatta points out the need to take into account both the confidence and enthusiasm of the staff and the receptivity of the community in evaluating the results of an evaluation study. He suggests that "either enthusiasm of the staff or the receptivity of the community may make a program successful, when its procedures may not be effective as such. Further, both these factors may lead to a favorable evaluation of the program, independently of whether it has been effective or not. Under such circumstances, each program must be viewed as a single case."[35]

On the broadest level, we may evaluate the "input" or stimulus variable in terms of the organizational structure and function of the agency carrying out the program. Basically, such organizational evaluations underlie the comprehensive evaluation guides put out by the American Public Health Association's Committee on Administrative Practices as discussed in Chapter II. Concentrating as these evaluative instruments do on "effort," the independent or causal variable of "input" tends to become at the same time the dependent or effect variable. This overlap points to one of the basic fallacies of this type of administrative evaluation. Effort tends to become substituted for accomplishment.[36] Several sophisticated models for organizational evaluation have been offered by Simon in terms of factors affecting "decision-making,"[37] and by Blau and Scott, as well as others, utilizing a social system orientation which views the organization as a system of mutually dependent parts.[38] We will return to this aspect of evaluation in more detail in the chapters on administrative factors.

The concept of process is crucial to an understanding of the problems involved in isolating and controlling the program variables hypothesized as causes of the desired effect. As indicated previously, we may conceive of a set of preconditions which influence the program we set up (and therefore have "causal" significance for any subsequent effects) and of a set of intervening variables which occur between the independent and the dependent variable. However, in the chain of events from precondition of the program to consequences of the effects, what one calls the independent or dependent variables is largely a matter of which segment of this continuous causal chain is selected for study.

In program evaluation, it is imperative to select a segment which embodies the essential aspects of one's program. Thus, the preconditions will usually be limited in time to those that have immediate bearing upon the current program, with the others being relegated to a secondary position of historic interest. The independent variable will usually emphasize those aspects of the program which one feels are particularly significant and, in an evaluation, which are more or less manipulable. Greater interest will be attached to those parts of the program over which one has control and, especially, those which one may deliberately change for evaluative purposes.

Other criteria affecting the selection of the independent program variable to be evaluated will be the resources available for introducing change—some aspects of a program would cost more to change and might involve long-term staff recruitment and training programs; sensitivity to change—some parts of a program provide better openings for change than others; and complexity of interdependence—some parts of a program are so highly integrated with others that no change is possible without completely disrupting the entire existing program. It is, of course, important to keep in mind that the basic objective of the evaluation is usually not to determine how well the program operates, but how effectively it attains its goals.

Intervening variable analysis in evaluative research has the same general purpose as in basic research: (1) to test the "spuriousness" of one's attribution of effectiveness to the independent program variable; (2) to elaborate upon conditions which modify the effectiveness of the program; and (3) to specify the process whereby the program leads to the desired effect. We cannot here go into the rather technical details of intervening variable analysis. These are presented in several textbooks and articles on research methodology.[39] Suffice it to say here that this form of analysis can do much toward overcoming the difficulty in evaluative research of first isolating the stimulus to be tested and then controlling its administration as one can in the experimental laboratory. As Cattell indicates, "The controlled, univariate experiment, in which nothing but the independent variable alters to an important degree, becomes inapplicable and obsolete. . . . But multivariate statistical designs do more than provide an effective way of handling what used to be called the controlled variable and the uncontrolled variable in situations where control is impossible."[40]

3. *Definition and Measurement of Criteria of Effect—The Dependent Variable.* In nonevaluative research, the dependent variable usually designates the phenomenon being investigated, be it heart disease, juvenile delinquency, or poverty. Hypotheses are usually formulated in terms of

factors and conditions affecting the appearance of this phenomenon. In evaluative research, on the other hand, the focus of attention is more likely to be upon the program or activity being evaluated—the independent variable discussed above, with hypotheses being formulated in terms of the factors and conditions affecting the successful carrying-out of this program or activity.[41] The methodological questions to be discussed in the present section revolve around the problem of defining what is meant by success and how may it be measured.

Defining the Dependent Variable. A crucial question in evaluative research is, "What do we mean by a successful result?" All programs will have some effects, but how do we measure these effects and how do we determine whether they are the particular effects we are interested in producing? As in the case of the independent program variables, we note a multiplicity and interdependence of effect variables. Again our main problem is one of selecting from among the myriad of possible effects, those most relevant to our objectives.

We have already noted five major criteria for determining relevance: (1) effort or activity; (2) performance or accomplishment; (3) adequacy or impact; (4) efficiency or output relative to input; and (5) process or specification of conditions of effectiveness. In a sense we may classify the first two criteria as *evaluative*, that is, concerned with the determination of the relationship between activities and effects; the second two as *administrative*, dealing with a judgment about the size and cost of the effort relative to the effects; while the last one is really a *research* criterion, concerned with increased knowledge or understanding irrespective of effect.

Indices for the first two, effort and performance, are likely to be defined by the public service worker in terms of professional standards; the next two, adequacy and efficiency, are more likely to be determined by the administrator in terms of organizational goals and practices; the last one, process, is largely an evaluation made by the academician or researcher in terms of basic knowledge. To a large extent, the formulation of the objectives and design of an evaluative research project will depend upon who is conducting the project and what use will be made of the results.

Ballard and Mudd raise the issue of "Whose judgment of improvement, then, represents the most appropriate measure of the effectiveness of treatment?"[42] They distinguish at least four evaluating agents in relation to counseling programs whose definition of effectiveness might differ: (1) the client; (2) the persons closely related to the client; (3) society in general; and (4) the counselor. These four groups often formulate different sets of criterion measures, perhaps related, but certainly not identical and perhaps even in opposition, and, most important, each with its own validity.

This problem of the validity of criteria of effectiveness is crucial to evaluative research. These criteria represent the observable operational indices for measuring the attainment of program objectives. To some degree they should satisfy the requirements of construct validity as well as the more technical conditions of index reliability and predictive validity. Wallace formulates this issue in terms of utility versus understanding. He argues against the point of view that "validation for instruments employed in diagnosis and therapy is unnecessary so long as they provide the clinician with a sense of security about what he is doing." He goes on to state that "it is as important to gain insight into why our procedures do or do not work as it is to produce a tried-and-true predictive gimmick."[43]

This approach to criteria of effectiveness in terms of more general concepts as opposed to specific operational measures is endorsed by Miller, who discusses some of the pitfalls involved in evaluation studies which concentrate upon single, specific activities and effects. He strongly recommends the manipulation of variables by a variety of techniques and the measurement of the consequent effects by a variety of criteria.[44] This is related to the same problem discussed in the section on research design in terms of the greater generalizability of variable testing compared with program testing. Just as we gain in understanding and control by viewing our "causal" variables in broader terms, we also gain by defining our "effect" variables in terms of more general concepts of a class of objectives.

Emphasis on evaluative criteria which have greater construct validity will do much to move public service program objectives away from purely operational goals of certain activities to the ultimate objectives. Thus, we would be concerned with how many nurse visits were made, or how often a woman attended a prenatal clinic, or whether someone reads a pamphlet on the signs of cancer only insofar as these criteria were valid steps toward the health improvement we wished to produce. In a sense we must show that these effects (dependent variables) are actually causes (independent variables) or intermediary steps (intervening variables) toward an ultimate objective.

The final methodological problem in evaluative research concerns the measurement of the dependent variable, or the effects of the public service or social action program. Once the criteria of success have been defined, the research task becomes one of observing and measuring these criteria in a reliable and valid manner. This problem of criteria measurement is crucial for evaluative research, since no evaluation can be made in the absence of some standard by which to judge success or failure. The following chapter deals with this problem in some detail.

NOTES TO CHAPTER VI

1. Suchman, Edward A., "The Principles of Research Design," in Doby, John T., and others, *An Introduction to Social Research.* The Stackpole Co., Harrisburg, Pa., 1954, p. 254.

2. Good discussions of research design are given in Ackoff, Russell L., *The Design of Social Research,* University of Chicago Press, Chicago, 1953; Cornfield, Jerome, and William Haenszel, "Some Aspects of Retrospective Studies," *Journal of Chronic Diseases,* vol. 11, May, 1960, pp. 523–534; Rosenstock, Irwin M., and Godfrey M. Hochbaum, "Some Principles of Research Design in Public Health," *American Journal of Public Health,* vol. 51, February, 1961, pp. 266–277; Miller, Delbert, editor, *Handbook of Research Design and Social Measurement,* David McKay Co., New York, 1964.

3. Greenberg, Bernard G., and Berwyn F. Mattison, "The Whys and Wherefores of Program Evaluation," *Canadian Journal of Public Health,* vol. 46, July, 1955, pp. 298–299.

4. Campbell, D. T., "Factors Relevant to the Validity of Experiments in Social Settings," *Psychological Bulletin,* vol. 54, 1957, pp. 297–312; Campbell, D. T., and J. C. Stanley, "Experimental and Quasi-Experimental Designs for Research on Teaching," in Gage, N. L., editor, *Handbook of Research on Teaching,* Rand McNally and Co., Chicago, 1963, pp. 171–246.

5. Stouffer, Samuel A., "Some Observations on Study Design," *American Journal of Sociology,* vol. 55, January, 1950, pp. 355–361.

6. For example, Cochran reports the following reaction of a number of doctors who responded to a questionnaire on smoking and lung cancer by saying, "I have been smoking twenty cigarettes a day, but after reading this questionnaire, I have given up smoking forever." Cochran, William G., "Research Techniques in the Study of Human Beings," *Milbank Memorial Fund Quarterly,* vol. 33, 1955, p. 132.

7. Solomon, Richard L., "An Extension of Control Group Design," *Psychological Bulletin,* vol. 46, March, 1949, pp. 137–150.

8. Modell, Walter, and Raymond W. Houde, "Factors Influencing Clinical Evaluation of Drugs," *Journal of the American Medical Association,* vol. 167, August 30, 1958, p. 2191. See also Beecher, H. K. "Powerful Placebo," *Journal of the American Medical Association,* vol. 159, December 24, 1955, pp. 1602–1606.

9. Actually, there may also be a "negative" placebo action in the case of patients who lack faith in doctors or drugs, or who have a need to remain

or become ill. Evidence for this can be seen in studies reporting "toxic" effects on the part of subjects receiving placebo treatments. See, for example, Wolf, Stewart, and R. H. Pinsky, "Effects of Placebo Administration and Occurrence of Toxic Reactions, *Journal of the American Medical Association*, vol. 155, May 22, 1954, pp. 339–341.

10. One evaluation, for example, showed that the attitudes of clinicians to mental illness and the use of chemotherapy have a significant relationship to patient improvement, as determined by independent observers. Honigfeld, Gilbert, "Relationships Among Physicians' Attitudes and Response to Drugs," *Psychological Reports*, vol. 11, December, 1962, pp. 683–690.

11. Shapiro, A. K., "The Placebo Effect in the History of Medical Treatment: Implications for Psychiatry," *American Journal of Psychiatry*, vol. 116, October, 1959, pp. 298–304.

12. Frank, Jerome D., *Persuasion and Healing*. Johns Hopkins Press, Baltimore, 1961, p. 66.

13. James, George, *Evaluation in Public Health*. Department of Health, New York City, p. 7. Mimeographed, n.d.

14. Webster's New Intercollegiate Dictionary, 1957 edition.

15. Reader, George G., and Mary E. W. Goss, "The Sociology of Medicine," in Merton, Robert K., Leonard Broom, and Leonard S. Cottrell, Jr., editors, *Sociology Today: Problems and Prospects*. Basic Books, New York, 1959, p. 242.

16. Fisher, Ronald A., *The Design of Experiments*, Oliver and Boyd, Edinburgh, Scotland, 1937; Chapin, F. Stuart, *Experimental Designs in Sociological Research*, Harper and Bros., New York, 1947; Cochran, W. G. and G. M. Cox, *Experimental Designs*, John Wiley and Sons, New York, 1950.

17. Wier, J. M., and others, "An Evaluation of Health and Sanitation in Egyptian Villages," *Journal of the Egyptian Public Health Association*, vol. 27, 1952, pp. 55–114.

18. Meyer, Henry J., and Edgar F. Borgatta, *An Experiment in Mental Patient Rehabilitation*. Russell Sage Foundation, New York, 1959, pp. 105–106.

19. A control group could be added to the design, as follows, to check on the effects of previous exposures upon the experimental group.

$$O_1 \ X_1 \ O_2 \ X_2 \ O_3 \ X_3 \ O_4$$
$$O_5$$
$$O_6$$
$$O_7$$

This type of design was used in Lazarsfeld, Paul F., Bernard Berelson, and Hazel Gaudet, *The People's Choice*, Columbia University Press, New York, 1948.

20. Dawber, Thomas A., William B. Kannel, and Lorna P. Lytell, "An Approach to Longitudinal Studies in a Community: The Framingham Study," *Annals of the New York Academy of Sciences*, vol. 107, May 22, 1963, pp. 539–556; Zeisel, Hans, *Say It with Figures*, Harper and Bros., New York, 1947, chap. 10.

21. Pelz, Donald, and Frank M. Andrews, "Detecting Causal Priorities in

Panel Study Data," *American Sociological Review*, vol. 28, December, 1964, pp. 836–848.

22. For a concise analysis of experimental design problems present in conducting both applied and basic research, see Edwards, Allen L., and Lee J. Cronback, "Experimental Design for Research in Psychotherapy," *Journal of Clinical Psychology*, vol. 8, January, 1952, pp. 51–59. Discussions of the formal logical requirements of evaluative research may be found in MacMahon, Brian, Thomas F. Pugh, and George B. Hutchison, "Principles in the Evaluation of Community Mental Health Programs," *American Journal of Public Health*, vol. 51, July, 1961, pp. 963–968; and Glidewell, J. C., "Methods for Community Mental Health Research," *American Journal of Orthopsychiatry*, vol. 27, January, 1957, pp. 38–54.

23. Cochran, William G., "Methodological Problems in the Study of Human Populations," *Annals of the New York Academy of Sciences*, vol. 107, May 22, 1963, p. 476.

24. An excellent "sampling chart" comparing the advantages and disadvantages of different sampling designs may be found in Ackoff, Russell L., *op. cit.*, pp. 124–125. See also Cochran, William G., *Sampling Techniques*, John Wiley and Sons, New York, 1953.

25. Blenkner, M., "Obstacles to Evaluative Research in Casework," *Social Casework*, vol. 31, March, 1950, p. 98.

26. Hyman, Herbert H., Charles R. Wright, and Terence K. Hopkins, *Applications of Methods of Evaluation: Four Studies of the Encampment for Citizenship*. University of California Press, Berkeley, 1962, pp. 23–24.

27. Rogers, Carl, and R. F. Dymond, editors, *Psychotherapy and Personality Change*. University of Chicago, Chicago, 1954.

28. Borgatta, Edgar F., "Research: Pure and Applied," *Group Psychotherapy*, vol. 8, October, 1955, pp. 263–277.

29. Meyer, Henry J., and Edgar F. Borgatta, *op. cit.*

30. Smith, M. Brewster, "Evaluation of Exchange of Persons," *International Social Science Bulletin*, vol. 7, no. 3, 1955, p. 391.

31. Mathen, K. K., "Matching in Comparative Studies in Public Health," *Indian Journal of Public Health*, vol. 7, 1963, pp. 161–169. See also Cochran, William G., "Matching in Analytical Studies," *American Journal of Public Health*, vol. 43, June, 1953, pp. 684–691.

32. Dunbar, Flanders, *Psychiatry in the Medical Specialties*. McGraw-Hill, Inc., New York, 1959.

33. Hyman, Herbert H., and others, *op. cit.*, p. 75.

34. Jacob, Phillip E., *Changing Values in College*, Harper and Bros., New York, 1957; Barton, Allen H., *Studying the Effects of College Education*, The Edward W. Hazen Foundation, New Haven, 1959.

35. Borgatta, Edgar F., "Research Problems in Evaluation of Health Service Demonstrations," *Milbank Memorial Fund Quarterly*, vol. 44, October, 1966, part 2, p. 197.

36. See Chapter IV for an analysis of the difference between "effort" and "accomplishment" as evaluative criteria.

37. Simon, Herbert A., *Administrative Behavior*. Macmillan Co., New York, 1957.

38. Blau, Peter M., and W. Richard Scott, *Formal Organizations.* Chandler Publishing Co., San Francisco, 1961.
39. Lazarsfeld, Paul F., "Interpretation of Statistical Relations as a Research Operation," in Lazarsfeld, Paul F., and Morris Rosenberg, editors, *The Language of Social Research,* The Free Press, Glencoe, Ill., 1955, pp. 115–125; Hyman, Herbert, *Survey Design and Analysis,* The Free Press, Glencoe, Ill., 1955; Zetterberg, Hans L., *On Theory and Verification in Sociology,* The Bedminster Press, Totowa, N.J., 1963. See also Simon, Herbert A., "Spurious Correlation: A Causal Interpretation," *Journal of the American Statistical Association,* vol. 49, September, 1954, pp. 467–479, Blalock, Hubert M., Jr., "Evaluating the Relative Importance of Variables," *American Sociological Review,* vol. 26, December, 1961, pp. 866–874.
40. Cattell, Raymond B., *Learning Theory, Personality Theory and Clinical Research.* John Wiley and Sons, New York, 1954.
41. A corollary of this distinction between nonevaluative and evaluative hypotheses concerns the interpretation of "significant." In nonevaluative research, an independent variable is deemed to have a significant *relationship* to the dependent variable if the size of the observed association surpasses what might have been expected by chance alone. This is statistical significance. In evaluative research, an independent variable is interpreted as having a significant *effect* upon the dependent variable if the observed change is judged administratively desirable. This is program significance. Statistical significance relates only to sampling error while program significance is usually determined by an input-output equation of impact relative to cost. Chapin notes the foregoing distinction in terms of the difference between verification (nonevaluative) and vindication (evaluative). "Both promoter and administrator are tempted when making a judgment of the importance of a gain associated with a social program to substitute the psychology of vindication for the psychology of verification; to substitute the notion of justification of a position taken in advance and expressed by emotional appeal for the operation of confirming the results of applying a program by repetition of the program under like conditions. Thus is the spirit of vindication unconsciously substituted for the spirit of verification." Chapin, F. Stuart, *Experimental Designs in Sociological Research.* Harper and Bros., New York, 1947, p. 177.
42. Ballard, Robert G., and Emily H. Mudd, "Some Theoretical and Practical Problems in Evaluating Effectiveness of Counseling," *Social Casework,* vol. 38, December, 1957, p. 534.
43. Wallace, S. Rains, "Criteria for What?" *American Psychologist,* vol. 20, June, 1965, pp. 416–417.
44. Miller, Neal E., "Analytical Studies of Drive and Reward," *American Psychologist,* vol. 16, December, 1961, pp. 739–754.

CHAPTER VII

The Measurement of Effects

Our conceptual analysis of the meaning of the dependent or effect variable in evaluative research reinforces the basic point made in Chapter IV, Types and Categories of Evaluation, that the measurement of the effects of a program requires specification according to four major categories of variables: (1) component parts or processes of the program; (2) specific population or target groups reached; (3) situational conditions within which the program occurs; and (4) differential effects of the program.[1] The methodological problems involved in providing for the collection of data on the first three aspects have been discussed in terms of the isolation and control of the independent or program variable and the sampling of equivalent experimental and control groups. In this chapter we would like to concentrate upon measurement problems arising from differential effects.

First, a word about measurement, in general, as this applies to the determination of the *reliability* and *validity* of the criteria of effectiveness. The criteria in evaluative research create measurement problems similar to those of operational indices for nonevaluative research. For the most part, the research worker does not measure the phenomena he is studying directly. Rather he observes and measures empirical manifestations or indices of these phenomena. "It is not the criteria themselves which are tested or measured, but their equivalents. . . . Whatever the indicators tentatively selected—and they will tend to vary with the individual study —their logical and psychological nexus with program objectives and the criteria of their achievement must be demonstrated."[2] Lazarsfeld and Rosenberg deal with this problem in some detail in terms of two basic questions: (1) How does one "think up" indicators for the criteria being studied? (2) How does one select from all possible indicators, those to be used for any particular purpose?[3]

Technically, two major methodological procedures exist for evaluating the success with which one has measured criteria of effectiveness. These are the basic methodological concepts of reliability and validity. While a great deal has been written about these concepts, they are still subject to frequent misunderstanding, especially in relation to evaluative research.

In general, public service and social action research are deficient in their concern with the reliability and validity of their evaluative instruments.[4]

Elinson maintains, "Very few reliability studies have been done in medicine. . . . It is as if to question the reliability of a medical measure is to interfere with the practice of medicine (have confidence in your doctor)."[5] He mentions one study which found that of two physicians with similar training, one physician was able to find 50 per cent more cases of a disease in equivalent random samples of patients.[6] The importance of reliability is generally acknowledged by statisticians and epidemiologists being accorded first place by the World Health Organization among a current list of research requirements.

As described by Moore, "Every study should make some provision for tests of reproducibility of at least selected types of measurements on samples of subjects throughout the course of the study. The essential factor in such tests is the independent application, by two or more persons, of the same procedure to the same object or study, whether the object of study be a specimen or serum, an x-ray film, or a subject's description of his symptoms."[7] This problem of a reliable measure of the observable indices of criteria of effect is as important for evaluation studies as it is for any form of research.

The reliability of a measure refers to the degree to which this measure can be depended upon to secure consistent results upon repeated application. Reliability, therefore, indicates the probability of obtaining the same results upon repeated use of the same measuring instrument whether this be an objective test or a subjective judgment. This criterion represents the dependability or stability aspect of an evaluation. Traditionally, reliability has been limited to a measure of random unsystematic error only; that is, the variation in response obtained by chance alone from one trial to another. The inconsistent results indicative of low reliability are produced by such unsystematic error. The results of a systematic error might still be consistent, and therefore reliable. This type of chance variation is present in *all* evaluation and constitutes an important aspect of any measuring instrument or procedure.

Zetterberg discusses four different types of reliability: (1) the congruence of several indicators or the extent to which several indicators measure the same thing; (2) the precision of an instrument or the extent to which the same indicator is consistent for a single observer; (3) the objectivity of an instrument or the extent to which the same indicator is consistent for two or more observers; and (4) the constancy of the object measured or the extent to which the object being measured does not fluctuate. Zetterberg concludes, "The variance between indicators reveals congruency; the variance between readings indicates precision; the variance between observers indicates objectivity; the variance between different times indicates constancy."[8]

Reliability is a necessary condition for validity. An evaluative measure which cannot be depended upon to give the same results upon repetition because of large random errors obviously cannot be used to measure anything and therefore cannot have any validity. However, a reliable measure may still have low validity; that is, although the measures are consistent, they do not deal with the "right" criterion. Moore speaks of the "Substitution Game" in which such measures as "blood pressure level" are substituted for "hypertensive disease" or "serum cholesterol level" for "coronary artery disease."[9] On a more general level in public service programs, such substitution takes place when we evaluate effort expended instead of results accomplished.

A complicating factor in the measurement of the reliability of an evaluative instrument is the problem of actual change. A measure which produces different results upon repetition may indicate that a change has taken place and not that the measure is unreliable. Thus, a reliable evaluative instrument measuring valid change might appear unreliable. Elinson points out the following paradox: "If what one observes is highly variable by nature (blood pressure, a mood, the position of an electron), how can one tell whether differences in repeated measurements are due to change in the observed phenomenon or to unreliability of the method of observation?"[10]

There is a basic confusion in most discussions of reliability between variation due to chance or random errors and variation due to inconsistent measures. Inconsistency of measurement may be due to a great many other factors besides chance error. In the traditional sense, a measuring instrument is unreliable if it possesses a great deal of chance variation; that is, repeated readings from the instrument will vary at random beyond an acceptable level of consistency. The supposition is that there is some "true" value about which the readings of the instrument fluctuate because of chance errors. The degree of preciseness desired and the range of fluctuation permissible will determine the reliability of the instrument.

In evaluation, reliability is affected not only by chance errors of the measuring instrument, but also by actual fluctuations of the object being measured. In this sense the "true" value of the measurement is itself subject to a range of variability and a "reliable" instrument should indicate this variability. Thus, Clark and his associates have shown how blood pressure readings may vary under different conditions,[11] while similar findings exist in relation to electrocardiogram readings[12] and psychiatric diagnoses.[13] Whether one calls this validity or reliability will depend upon the extent to which one wishes to limit the concept of reliability to its traditional use as a measure of random or chance variation alone. In the present discussion of reliability, the emphasis will be upon those factors in evaluation which tend to produce inconsistency of measurements in a more or less random or unsystematic manner. Nonrandom inconsistency will be treated under validity.

Sources of Unreliability. It is important in analyzing reliability of measures of change due to public service or social action programs to distinguish between those differences in measurement which result from a "true" change and those which reflect instrumental inconsistencies. Perhaps the most useful distinction can be made between random inconsistency and systematic inconsistency. Where it can be shown that the differences in results obtained at different times appear to follow no logically consistent pattern, we may speak of such results as lacking reliability. Where it can be shown, however, that the variations in results follow meaningful patterns, or can be attributed to other than chance factors, we could probably more profitably analyze such difference in terms of significant change. The correct interpretation of "inconsistency" in this case is really a problem in validity.

Let us limit our present analysis of reliability, therefore, simply to those sources of inconsistency which we have reason to believe are largely due to random or chance factors. The major sources of such unsystematic variation in evaluative research are:

1. Subject reliability—the subject's mood, motivation, fatigue, and so on —may momentarily affect his physical and mental health and his attitudes and behavior in relation to public service programs. When such factors are of a transient nature, they may produce unsystematic changes in his responses.

2. Observer reliability—the same personal factors will also affect the way in which an observer makes his measurements. These observer factors will not only tend to affect the subject's reactions, but also the observer's interpretation of the subject's responses.

3. Situational reliability—the conditions under which the measurement is made—may produce changes in results which do not reflect "true" changes in the population being studied. If the variation in the evaluation situation is systematic, one could then, of course, make valid deductions about the effect of the evaluation situation upon one's measure. However, if such variation is random, then these situational factors will not produce any constant bias (which perhaps could be corrected to produce valid results) but rather unsystematic responses which produce unreliable results.

4. Instrument reliability—all of the aforementioned factors will combine to produce an evaluative instrument of low reliability. However, certain specific aspects of the instrument itself may affect its reliability. Poorly worded questions in an interview, for example, especially those which are ambiguous or double-barreled, may lead to a random variation in responses.

5. Processing reliability—simple coding or mechanical errors when they occur at random or in an unsystematic manner may also lead to a lack of reliability.

Since all measurement contains some error, the problem for evaluation is to reduce the error to such a degree that it does not interfere with the valid use of the evaluative instrument. There is no absolute level which distinguishes a reliable measure from an unreliable one. The use to which the results of the measurement are put will determine whether the obtained degree of reliability is sufficiently high. Reliability has its greatest effects upon the precision of measurement—the more precise the measure desired, the more important will reliability be—and upon the size of relationships or significance of differences between groups—the more important it is to know the degree of difference, the more attention must be paid to unreliability.

Since unreliability is due to random or chance error, such error may often be cancelable. Errors in one direction will be made as frequently as errors in the other direction, so that the empirical measurements will still validly reflect the objective situation. However, while overall reliability may still be high in such a case, individual subject reliability will remain low and of considerable consequence in any type of analysis involving correlation or cross tabulation, either analytical or predictive. Since a great deal of evaluative research requires the use of cross-tabulations, reliability constitutes a serious problem for the evaluation study. This problem was recognized by Moore who concluded, "Individual biological variability is much more difficult to evaluate than simple laboratory reproducibility, yet it may be much more important in intraindividual comparisons in longitudinal studies. There is need for more complete documentation of individual variability for many widely used measures."[14]

Reliability can best be controlled through careful attention to those factors which permit large chance errors to enter into the evaluation measurement. Such unreliability often results from carelessness and inadequate precautions against unsystematic error. Since it is known that some error must occur, it is important to provide checks upon the size of this error. For the most part, however, in evaluative research the major problem will not be one of reliability, but of validity. If the results of a study are shown to be valid as discussed below, the reliability of the evaluative instrument may largely be taken for granted.

VALIDITY

Validity is by far the most important single methodological criterion for evaluating any measuring instrument, evaluative or nonevaluative. As Herzog points out, "The problem of validity invades every aspect and every detail of the evaluative process, especially the selection, definition, and application of criteria."[15] Validity refers to the degree to which any measure or procedure succeeds in doing what it purports to do. From this definition it is obvious that until the objective of a program can be specified and some reliable criterion for measuring success of failure provided, it will not be possible to conduct a meaningful test of validity.

Validity reflects those errors which are systematic or constant. To be systematic, these errors must represent some form of "bias" which slants the results in a particular direction rather than at random. The factors affecting the validity of results may therefore be viewed as "causal" and may constitute an important source of analysis in themselves.

Validity refers to the "meaning" of an evaluative measure or an operation. The relevance of the measure for interpretation is in this sense determined by its validity. The "meaning" of the measure is, in turn, determined by the "purpose" for which the measure has been designed. The "purpose" is measured by the extent to which the measure relates to some given criterion. We may distinguish the following types of criterion of relevance for validity:

(a) Face validity. This is the basic measure that the evaluator himself has decided upon. He justifies his choice in terms of the "obvious" significance of the measure.

(b) Consensual validity. A type of face validity is the use of expert judgment. It is the same as (a) above, only rather than one judge, it involves the consensus of a panel of experts.

(c) Correlational or criterion validity. Here one correlates a measure with something else that one "knows" measures it. "What one knows measures it" is, of course, simply a statement of relevance or face or construct validity. If the two correlate highly, the measure has validity.

(d) Predictive validity. The correlation of present measures with something that takes place in the future. Predictive validity will vary with what is being predicted and with other circumstances which may obtain. For example, we *define* what we mean by weight (face validity). We observe that heavy people occupy more room than light people, and we put people on a bench and observe that there is a correlation between weight and the amount of room occupied (correlational validity). We predict that heavy people will die sooner than light people (predictive validity). It should be clear that there is room for error in substituting correlation or predictive validity for construct validity.

Relation to Reliability. Reliability and validity are closely interdependent. There can be no validity without reliability. However, one can have high reliability without validity. Since reliability is a necessary condition for validity, those chance or random factors which tend to lower reliability may also be viewed as causes of low validity. However, factors which create low validity may not affect the reliability of a measure or operation. Since one cannot secure high validity by means of measures which have low reliability, the presence of high validity may often be taken as indicative of a satisfactory degree of reliability. If we can show that a measure is valid, we can often take for granted that it is reliable.

While a single evaluative measure has only one reliability—that is, the extent to which the measure is stable is determined regardless of the use to which the measure is put—any single measure may have many different validities, depending upon the purpose for which the measure is used. Thus, a measure may easily be valid for one evaluation and invalid for another.

Validity presents a much broader problem than reliability. It refers not only to a specific measure, but also to the significance of the whole evaluation process from formulation of objectives through the collection of data to the interpretation of findings. The validity of an evaluation study refers not only to the validity of its specific criteria or measures, but also to the theory underlying the formulation of the hypotheses concerning the relationship of the activities to the objectives.

Factors Affecting Validity. Any factor, whether it be a specific measure, a procedure of administration, or a statement of objectives, which introduces a systematic error or "bias" into the conduct of the evaluation may be considered a source of invalidity. Bias affects validity because it slants the data away from some "objective" truth, either explicit or implicit. The recognition of such bias thus becomes an important problem for the increase of validity. If the bias is known, it may often be corrected. This correction may range from a simple caution to the reader to a systematic "adjustment" to eliminate the bias, especially where the relationship between the biased and unbiased results can be determined. In the latter case, the bias may actually be turned to an advantage if the biased results can be obtained with greater reliability and less cost.

Since validity is affected by bias, and since bias may occur at any and all stages in the evaluative research process, the problem of validity exists at all stages of the entire operation of an evaluative research project. Briefly, therefore, we have:

1. Propositional validity—the use of "wrong" theoretical assumptions or "biased" objectives. Invalid program objectives may spring from basically invalid theories or from invalid deductions from valid theories.

2. Instrument validity—the use of inappropriate or irrelevant operational indices. Given a valid index, one may still obtain an invalid measure of this index, because of such instrumental factors as biased readings or misunderstanding by the subject.

3. Sampling validity—the degree to which the sample of respondents included in the study represents the population from which they are chosen. Such representativeness may also be affected by "no response" through failure to reach an individual included in the sample.

4. Observer or evaluator validity—observers may introduce a consistent bias, depending upon their own beliefs or preconceived notions about the results in general, or the subject in particular. If the observer influences a subject in a constant direction, he may be said to have introduced a bias which lowers the validity of their response.

5. Subject validity—the habits of the individual being studied, his predisposition toward particular modes of expression may introduce "irrelevant" and, therefore, invalid biases into the specific content of the measures being made. At times deliberate misinformation by the subject will also decrease validity. This is likely to occur when the subject feels that his responses have some particular purpose and he himself would like to see the results of the evaluation used in a particular way. He may give invalid information where he is concerned with creating a favorable or

unfavorable appraisal of a situation, where he wishes to impress the evaluator rather than inform him, where he wishes deliberately to conceal certain confidential information, and so on.

6. Administration validity—the conditions under which an evaluation study is conducted may constitute a source of invalidity. Different methods of collecting data are known to produce different results. Field conditions may introduce systematic error, that is, trained versus untrained observers, the season of the year, the auspices of the study, and so on.

7. Analysis validity—the analyst, of course, is a key individual in determining the way in which data will be analyzed and interpreted. Aside from the obvious problem of deliberate bias in order to prove a preconceived point of view, we have the much more subtle bias of personal commitment to a particular program which in itself may be invalid.

The way in which the results are generalized to other programs either in a mistaken or overextended fashion may also lead one to label a study invalid. This type of invalidity would include the formulation of an invalid set of recommendations based upon the results of a particular study. If a study is directly intended to indicate a specific course of action, we may properly evaluate the forthcoming recommendations in terms of their validity, depending upon how well the action accomplished the desired goal. On a more technical level, spurious or invalid results may be obtained because of inadequate controls and the "wrong" choice of variables to be related. This is the invalidity of the so-called "spurious" attribution of an effect to some program activity which, while correlated, is not causually related.

Brogden and Taylor offer the following classification of sources of criterion invalidity in terms of "any variable, except errors of measurement and sampling error, producing a deviation of obtained criterion scores from a hypothetical 'true' criterion score."[16]

1. Criterion deficiency—omission of pertinent elements from the criterion.
2. Criterion contamination—introducing extraneous elements into the criterion.
3. Criterion scale-unit bias—inequality of scale units in the criterion.
4. Criterion distortion—improper weighting in combining criterion elements.

There are many examples of each of these sources of errors in evaluation studies of public service programs. We have already noted in Chapter II the extreme susceptibility of community services indices to each of the

four types of bias listed above. Such indices are likely to stress convenience and availability over validity and to include criteria which are irrelevant or only slightly associated with the major objective of a program,
while omitting others directly relevant but difficult to change or measure.
Similarly scale units and index weights are likely to be arbitrarily determined by subjective judgment rather than objective correlation. Ciocco
offers an excellent discussion of the weaknesses of most of these community indices in terms of both their low construct and operational validity.[17]
Fleck characterizes the use of such indices for public health program evaluation as serving a "ritualistic" function without offering any realistic
possibility of program change.[18]

In an analysis of the problem of validity in relation to evaluation studies,
Herzog suggests three levels or aspects of validation: "(1) Is the criterion
selected a valid criterion of what is to be measured (e.g., is improved job
performance a valid criterion of therapeutic gains); (2) Is the indicator
selected a valid reflector of the criterion (e.g., is increased production a
valid criterion of improved job performance); (3) Are the various valid
segments of the study combined in such a way as to preserve their individual validity and achieve validity of the whole?" In the absence of "objective" proof of improvement, criteria must be based upon "someone's conviction about what is desirable or undesirable, what is adjustment or
maladjustment, what is improvement or deterioration."[19] One study which
has served as a model of evaluation in mental health cites the following
common limitations in regard to validity: "A critical appraisal of our data
in terms of accuracy and reliability reveals the fact that . . . the material is
not only incomplete but is by no means unbiased."[20] Other reviews of
evaluations of psychiatric diagnosis and treatment programs also point to
a generally low level of validity.[21]

Tests of Validity. Since validity is judged in terms of purpose, it is
important in any test of validity to indicate some criterion of utility
against which validity can be appraised. There is no single test of validity
which can serve this purpose. Rather validity is built up through a series
of tests or arguments. These may range from the face validity of logical
reasoning to the predictive validity of a specific future event.

Most tests of validity involve the relationship which the measure being
tested has with some other measure. Where this relationship concerns
other measures which are hypothesized as having the same meaning as
the measure being tested, we may speak of the *internal validity* of the
measuring instrument. The purpose of such internal validity relates to the

definition of concepts and a definition is considered valid if it has high internal consistency; that is, if the various indices selected to measure this concept are all highly interrelated or related according to a preconceived model. To a large extent this is the type of validity one seeks in scaling procedures.

External validity, on the other hand, refers to the relationship between the test measure and some outside criterion. The better one can predict this outside criterion, the more validity one attributes to the test measure. On a simple level this may constitute nothing more than the comparison of the measure with some objective or factual criterion; for example, comparing how old a person says he is with his birth certificate. However, such validity is important only if the purpose of the study is the determination of the factual condition rather than the respondent's perception of it. To a large extent this type of external prediction of an objective measure of the same concept belongs to the classification above of internal validity.

The most significant test of validity for evaluation concerns *prediction,* which requires the theoretical formulation of a meaningful causal sequence. The validity of the measure is determined by hypothesizing which other independent measures might have "caused" the test measure or which outside dependent measures might be viewed as "effects" of the test measure. Thus, a measure is valid if we can predict preceding, subsequent, or related independent measures.

In this sense every meaningful correlation represents an association between two valid and reliable measures. If the reliability were too low, only a chance correlation would result. If the measures were invalid, the observed association would not make sense in terms of some predictive causal sequence. Thus, the basic analysis of validity must concern the "meaningfulness" of a relationship between the test measure and some independent or outside criterion. This applies equally to the relationship of an attitude to behavior or to another attitude. Whether behavior can be taken as an adequate criterion for the valid measurement of an attitude must depend upon the meaningfulness of the causal sequence between the attitude and the behavior.

Another test of validity consists of the subjective or judgmental evaluation of a measure as "making sense." Such validity depends upon securing agreement based upon judicial reasoning rather than the objective examination of a relationship between the measure and some criterion of validity. While this form of judgmental validity is extremely important in the early stages of program evaluation, it must sooner or later be subjected to the more rigorous tests of correlational or predictive validity.

Validity is a basic problem in all of science. It is inherent in all measurement, evaluative and nonevaluative. The best one can do is to attempt to increase validity: (1) by eliminating possible sources of invalidity and by increasing those factors which tend to produce unbiased measurement; (2) by including checks against which one may determine the degree of validity present; (3) by providing for corrections where the source of invalidity is known and can be adjusted in terms of the observed relationship between the invalid and the valid measure.

DIFFERENTIAL EFFECTS

As we have noted, all public service and action programs have multiple effects. Such differential effects will reflect the varying impacts of different segments of the total program, the variations in the target population which lead some groups to be more affected than others, the different times at which the effects may be measured, and the different situations or conditions under which the evaluation is made. Analysis of these differential effects will add much to one's understanding of why, where, and how a program failed or succeeded.

Perhaps the most significant aspect of these differential effects concerns a class of "unanticipated" or "unintended" effects. This phenomenon is well known in drug evaluation studies where there is a constant concern with negative side effects or contraindications. In relation to public health programs, Greenberg points out: "Declining maternal and infant death rates show that these programs have been 'successful,' but there is evidence that these savings in life have often been bought at the cost of increases in the numbers of blind, palsied, epileptic, and mentally deficient children."[22] Small suggests that the evaluative hypothesis, "Does activity 'A' reduce the frequency of morbidity 'M'?"; add the condition "and does it possibly increase the frequency of 'M₁,' 'M₂,' 'M₃'?"[23]

Social scientists have long been concerned with what Merton has called "the unanticipated consequences of purposive social action."[24] Social phenomena are so complex and interrelated that it is virtually impossible to change one facet without producing a series of other concomitant changes—both undesirable and desirable. "Boomerang" effects have been noted in almost all evaluations of "propaganda" or communication programs.[25] In any target population, there are bound to be some individuals who reject the desired message and react with greater antagonism or resistance. Bigman illustrates this point with an example from the field of public health. In a broadcast on the use of x-ray examinations and treatment by unlicensed practitioners, a radiologist repeatedly stressed the dangers of exposure to such an extent as to create unexpected anxieties which interfered with the legitimate use of such x-ray examinations and treatments.[26] Paul points out, in relation to mental hospitals, the danger of increasing guilt among relatives of hospitalized patients through a campaign stressing the "horrors" of many current mental institutions.[27]

These secondary effects of an action program are likely to be particularly disturbing when the program is intended to have some massive impact upon the society or community as a whole. This is particularly the case in regard to service or aid programs for the underdeveloped areas of the world. Opler describes this problem as follows in relation to the technical assistance program and points out the danger of too great a concern with possible negative side effects:

> The ideal situation, it was thought, would be one in which the technically appropriate task has been accomplished without accompanying complicating problems or with only such difficulties as have been anticipated, are controllable, and can be handled together. However, a warning was expressed that a look too far into such future contingencies might paralyze activity, and that some technical jobs are of such immediate and pressing importance that they should be undertaken without too much anticipation of accompanying tensions or intensified problems. It was felt that all plans are sure to have mixed consequences, and that such consequences should be and can be dealt with as they arise.[28]

Not all unintended effects are negative. Many evaluation studies have come up with findings of positive effects not originally anticipated. An example of such a "windfall" is given by Carlson in relation to a mass-information campaign on venereal disease. While Carlson failed to find any significant increase in volunteers for treatment, those counties exposed to the program showed an increase in the incidence of new cases being treated. He attributes this unanticipated benefit to the effect of the campaign upon the public health workers themselves which motivated them to more vigorous case-finding efforts.[29]

Knutson warns against the too-easy acceptance of unanticipated positive effects as justification for a program's existence. He states: "Such materials or programs should not be considered successful unless the intended objectives are also achieved. It matters not if the action caused is even more desirable than the action hoped for. To interpret as indications of success evidence of behavior changes other than those intended is to set up *post hoc* objectives."[30] While it may be possible to reformulate one's objectives in line with the unexpected findings, such a redefinition of the goals of the program would require a repetition of the evaluation study aimed specifically at these new goals.

Hyman suggests four ways of dealing with the unanticipated consequences of a program.

> First, for programs that have been in operation before, even though some consequences were unanticipated, they have nevertheless demonstrated themselves in previous cycles. . . . Second, an unanticipated consequence often is simply an extreme quantitative value of an intended effect, but at the extreme value it is transformed in its meaning. . . . Third, by distinguishing four types of effects of a program, one arrives at a rather bizarre type of unanticipated consequence. . . . An agency has anticipated certain effects which it regards as desirable and intends to achieve. . . . There are other unanticipated effects of the program, some of which, if recognized, would be regarded as desirable and others as undesirable. The fourth cell includes those effects which an agency might have originally anticipated as possible effects of its activities, but which are regarded as undesirable. These are the *anticipated unintended* objectives.[31]

These suggestions recognize that research is a learning process and that there is much to be learned from an evaluative study besides the simple test of effectiveness in achieving some specific objective. While such "research" uses of evaluation may not be of direct operational value, they can make a significant contribution to the growing field of public service administration.

Concern with an analysis of the differential effects of one's programs—which aspects of the total program were more effective, among which particular groups, at which times in the course of the program, and with what duration—provide the research material from which can be built general principles of public service administration as opposed to sets of operational instructions for running specific types of programs. Evaluation must be seen as one part of a general process including program research, planning, development, and operation. We shall address ourselves in more detail to this question in the next chapter on the relationship of evaluation to administration.

NOTES TO CHAPTER VII

1. This need to specify effects has been outlined by Getting and his associates as follows: "An objective must include the specifications of *who, where, when,* and *to what extent.* 'Who' refers to the target audience. Is the program directed at all people sick at home, only those referred by private physicians and hospitals, the indigent sick at home, or some other group? 'Where' concerns the geographical scope of the program. Is the program aimed at the target group in the agency's entire jurisdiction, in certain precincts or townships, or some other area? The 'What' refers to qualitative specificity. Is the desired effect that of rehabilitation, comfort, public relations, or some other consideration? The phrase 'to what extent' refers to the magnitude of the desired effect. Is it for the patient to meet the highest potential possible as judged by the attending physician? Is the patient expected to achieve a status that is satisfactory to him, even if less than his potential? Or is some other quantity of effect desired? Finally, specifying the 'when' indicates the time period thought necessary to achieve program goals." Getting, Vlado A., and others, "Research in Evaluation in Public Health Practices," Paper presented at the 92nd Annual Meeting of the American Public Health Association, New York, October 5, 1964, p. 12.
2. Bigman, Stanley K., "Evaluating the Effectiveness of Religious Programs," *Review of Religious Research,* vol. 2, Winter, 1961, pp. 108–109.
3. Lazarsfeld, Paul F., and Morris Rosenberg, editors, *The Language of Social Research.* The Free Press, Glencoe, Ill., 1955, p. 15.
4. For a good discussion of reliability and validity in relation to the measurement of the quality of medical care, see Donabedian, Avedis, "Evaluating the Quality of Medical Care," *Milbank Memorial Fund Quarterly,* vol. 44, part 2, July, 1966, pp. 166–203. Following a thorough analysis, he concludes, "The methods used may easily be said to have been of doubtful value and more frequently lacking in rigor and precision. . . . The process of evaluation itself requires much further study." (p. 191)
5. Elinson, Jack, "Methods of Socio-Medical Research," in Freeman, Howard, Sol Levine, and Leo G. Reeder, editors, *Handbook of Medical Sociology.* Prentice-Hall, Inc., Englewood Cliffs, N.J., 1963, p. 460.
6. Trussell, R. E., and Jack Elinson, *Chronic Illness in a Rural Area: The Hunterdon Study,* vol. 3. Harvard University Press, Cambridge, Mass., 1959.
7. Moore, Felix E., "Report of Committee on Design and Analysis of Studies," *American Journal of Public Health,* vol. 50, October, 1960, Supplement, p. 19.
8. Zetterberg, Hans L., *On Theory and Verification in Sociology.* The Bedminster Press, Totowa, N.J., 1963, pp. 50–51.
9. Moore, Felix E., *op. cit.,* p. 18.
10. Elinson, Jack, *op. cit.,* p. 459.

11. Clark, E. Gurney, Charles Y. Glock, Robert L. Vought, and Henry L. Lennard, "Studies in Hypertension, I–VI," *Journal of Chronic Diseases*, vol. 4, September and November, 1956, pp. 231–239, 469–498; vol. 5, February, 1957, pp. 174–196.

12. Commission on Chronic Illness, *Chronic Illness in a Large City: The Baltimore Study*, vol. 4. Harvard University Press, Cambridge, Mass., 1957.

13. Kreitman, N., "The Reliability of Psychiatric Diagnosis," *Journal of Mental Science*, vol. 107, September, 1961, pp. 876–886.

14. Moore, Felix E., *op. cit.*, p. 19.

15. Herzog, Elizabeth, *Some Guide Lines for Evaluative Research*. U.S. Department of Health, Education, and Welfare, Children's Bureau, Washington, 1959, p. 41.

16. Brodgen, Hubert E., and Erwin K. Taylor, "The Theory and Classification of Criterion Bias," *Educational and Psychological Measurement*, vol. 10, Summer, 1950, pp. 159–186.

17. Ciocco, Antonio, "On Indices for the Appraisal of Health Department Activities, *Journal of Chronic Diseases*, vol. 11, May, 1960, pp. 509–522.

18. Fleck, Andrew C., "Evaluation Research Programs in Public Health Practice," *Annals of the New York Academy of Sciences*, vol. 107, May 22, 1963, p. 721.

19. Herzog, Elizabeth, *op. cit.*, p. 44.

20. Miles, Henry H., Edna L. Barrabee, and Jacob E. Finesinger, "Evaluation of Psychotherapy," *Psychosomatic Medicine*, vol. 13, March–April, 1951, p. 103.

21. Eysenck, H. J., "The Effects of Psychotherapy: An Evaluation," *Journal of Consulting Psychology*, vol. 16, October, 1952, p. 319. See also Stevenson, Ian, "The Challenge of Results of Psychotherapy," *American Journal of Psychiatry*, vol. 116, August, 1959, pp. 120–123.

22. Gruenberg, Ernest M., "Application of Control Methods to Mental Illness," *American Journal of Public Health*, vol. 47, August, 1957, pp. 944–952.

23. *Planning Evaluations of Mental Health Programs*. Proceedings of the 34th Annual Conference of the Milbank Memorial Fund, New York, 1958, p. 50.

24. Merton, Robert K., "The Unanticipated Consequences of Purposive Social Action," *American Sociological Review*, vol. 1, December, 1936, pp. 894–904.

25. Lazarsfeld, Paul F., "Communication Research and the Social Psychologist," in Wayne, Dennis, and others, *Current Trends in Social Psychology*. University of Pittsburgh Press, Pittsburgh, 1948, pp. 218–273. Includes a bibliography.

26. Bigman, Stanley K., *op. cit.*, p. 110.

27. Paul, Benjamin D., editor, *Health, Culture, and Community*. Russell Sage Foundation, New York, 1955, p. 48.

28. Opler, Morris E., *Social Aspects of Technical Assistance in Operation*. Tensions and Technology Series, UNESCO, No. 4, Washington, 1954, p. 67.

29. Carlson, R. O., "The Influence of the Community and the Primary Group on the Reaction of Southern Negroes to Syphilis." Unpublished Ph.D. dissertation, Columbia University, 1952, pp. 246–247.
30. Knutson, Andie L., "Evaluating Health Education," *Public Health Reports*, vol. 67, January, 1952, p. 74.
31. Hyman, Herbert H., Charles R. Wright, and Terence K. Hopkins, *Applications of Methods of Evaluation: Four Studies of the Encampment for Citizenship.* University of California Press, Berkeley, 1962, pp. 12–13.

CHAPTER VIII

Evaluation and Program Administration

Evaluation is a form of programmatic activity in two major respects. First, the purpose of an evaluation is usually applied—its main objective is to increase the effectiveness of program administration. Second, the conduct of an evaluation study itself constitutes a form of program activity—the planning and execution of evaluation studies requires administrative resources. We might call the former evaluation *in* administration, while the latter could be classified as the administration *of* evaluation.

Evaluation as an aspect of program administration becomes an essential part of the entire administrative process related to program planning, development, and operation. In fact, as we shall see, it plays a central role in the growth of the new field of administrative science. At the same time, the conduct of evaluation studies, especially on a systematic, continuing basis, requires an administrative apparatus of its own and presents unique problems of organizational structure and function. In this chapter we will examine the first aspect of evaluation *in* program administration, while the next chapter will deal with the administration *of* evaluation studies of public service and social action programs.

EVALUATION AND ADMINISTRATIVE SCIENCE

Before looking specifically at the role of evaluation in program administration, let us examine briefly the concept of evaluation as a basic process in administrative science. Lewis offers the following useful proposition concerning the relationship of evaluation to knowledge and action: "Knowledge, action, and evaluation are essentially connected. The primary and pervasive significance of knowledge lies in its guidance of action: knowing is for the sake of doing. And action, obviously, is rooted in evaluation. For a being which did not assign comparative values, deliberate action would be pointless; and for one which did not know, it would be impossible."[1]

Thus, evaluative research as the study of planned social change supplies much of the knowledge base for the developing field of administrative science. The social experiment, involving the formulation and carrying out of programs designed to produce some desired change, is the main form of scientific research for the testing of administrative principles. Evaluative hypotheses are largely administrative hypotheses dealing with the relationship between some programmatic activity and the attainment of some desired action objective.

The evaluation study in social action is as essential to an empirically based administrative science as clinical or drug evaluation is to the practice of scientific medicine. In general, however, many administrators who may have done excellent work in measuring existing public needs, resources, and community attitudes, in following the general steps for defining objectives, and in carrying out of the requisite public service activity, seem unwilling to proceed with an evaluation of their efforts. If a need for a particular service appears to exist, then supplying that service in accord with the best available knowledge seems to them to be sufficient justification in itself. Thus, evaluation has not received the amount of attention it deserves from the field of public service as the basis for the formulation and development of policies of program administration.

Knutson is particularly critical of evaluation studies in the area of health education for neglecting these broader aspects of policy. He states: "The field of evaluation in health education is particularly weak in the program and policy design levels of research planning. If studies of evaluation are planned in terms of these broader frameworks, the evidence that accumulates will gradually satisfy the long-term as well as the short-term needs of health education and provide a sound basis for program planning."[2]

Evaluative research on a policy level has the important function of challenging traditional practices. James maintains, "Evaluation research is one of the few ways open to us for methodically changing the direction of our activities."[3] In particular, he distinguishes between programs of the past, present, and future.[4] Programs of the past are based upon needs which are well understood and accepted by both the professional and the community at large. In public health, for example, these constitute the traditional communicable disease programs, such as diptheria and smallpox. Public health activities in these areas need little further validation and the major problem is one of maintaining the existing barriers to these diseases. Evaluative research, however, can perform the worthwhile function of streamlining these activities and making them more efficient. Challenging the need for some of these programs through evaluation studies may also show that many of them have been oversold to the community and that changing conditions may have made them ineffective or even unnecessary. Thus, evaluation studies of past programs serve the valuable function of weeding out unproductive effort.

In regard to programs of the present, the need for such programs is also generally recognized, and while adequate resources may be available, they may not, as yet, be fully committed. Current programs do not have the established validity of programs of the past, but they do constitute acceptable targets for attack—even if only on a limited scale and with tentative backing. A significant problem still exists regarding the development of effective services for many current problems. Such programs in public health include tuberculosis control, infant and child supervision, dental programs, and health education in general. The greatest need for evaluation of these types of programs involves built-in evaluative research to assess current progress and to indicate promising new lines of attack. Such evaluation studies may also help to secure support for personnel and financial resources needed to meet existing problems.

Programs of the future are ill-defined except in general terms. Community services are scarce, developmental in nature, and inadequate in terms of the social problem. Similarly, community attitudes are unknown or generally apathetic. Examples of such problem areas in public health include accidents, heart disease, mental illness, cancer, and diabetes. Important as these problems are today as major causes of illness and death, effective public health activities remain to be developed in the future.

Evaluative research has a major contribution to make toward defining objectives and developing new control programs for the future. Demonstration programs of an experimental nature and incorporating evaluative research designs can serve five important functions: (1) to measure the impact of new activities upon the specific social problem; (2) to show their impact upon the other programs and activities of the service agency; (3) to test their acceptance by the public; (4) to serve as a framework for further research; and (5) to help the gradual development of future programs. Such evaluations of demonstration programs constitute perhaps one of the most important research activities of operating agencies.

Evaluation as part of the administrative process is closely tied to such important administrative functions as program planning, development, and operation. We usually think of evaluation as coming at the end of a sequence which proceeds as follows:

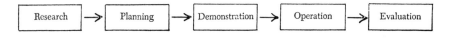

However, in a general sense, evaluation as a study of effectiveness may occur at each stage of this process. We may evaluate the findings of a research study, the proposals of a planning project, the feasibility of a developmental program, the accomplishments of an operational program, and even the significance of an evaluation study. It is important to keep in mind our definition of evaluation as the study of the desirable and undesirable consequences of planned social change and to recognize that each of the steps in the diagram above represents a form of human activity designed to achieve certain valued objectives, and, hence, subject to evaluative research.

RESEARCH

More specifically, each stage of the administrative process does present somewhat different problems for evaluation. Research programs raise both basic and applied problems of evaluation. As a form of basic research, they are subject to evaluation according to scientific criteria of study design, the reliability and validity of the measurements made, and the significance of the inferences or generalizations. The canons of the scientific method represent evaluative criteria for judging the success or failure of a research project.

Even as scientific projects, moreover, research programs may still be evaluated in terms of administrative criteria of input versus output. From the point of view of administrative science, however, the main criteria for evaluating research will usually relate to its *utility* to the administrator or program director. A great deal has been written about the problems of evaluating how well or poorly the findings of a research project have been utilized.[5] An oft-quoted remark is, "The road to inaction is paved with research reports."

Merton's discussion of "gaps" between research and policy is relevant here. He finds that (1) the research may not have been adequately focused on the practical problem, and (2) concrete forecasts may have been contingent upon uncontrolled conditions.[6] To these inherent "research" gaps must be added a wide range of "organizational" or "interpersonal" gaps between research and policy, that is, "the framework of values (organizational) precludes examination of some practicable courses of action"; "the policy-maker may be more willing to take the risks involved in decisions based on past experience than risks found in research-based recommendations"; "limitations of time and funds may at times condemn an applied research to practical futility"; "lack of continuing communication between policy-maker and research staff"; "status of researcher vis-à-vis the operating agency." This enumeration of barriers to successful research utilization is directly applicable to evaluative research as a form of applied research. We will view this problem in more detail in the next chapter when we discuss the administration *of* evaluative research projects.

PLANNING

In regard to program planning, evaluation is absolutely essential at all stages of the planning process. Planning proceeds step by step and each step must be evaluated before the next step can be taken. This principle is the basis of a rather ambitious attempt to make the planning process a systematic one involving the development of a network of events or activities related to each other along a time dimension and evaluated according to different estimates of resources and objectives. Known as PERT, this program for systematic planning has been applied to a wide range of administrative activities ranging from airplane production to classroom instruction.[7]

The First National Conference on Evaluation in Public Health assigned an important role to evaluation during program planning. Such evaluation should be built into any planning activity in order to provide for a check on the adequacy of the plan and to permit redirection before the plan becomes too fixed. During this planning stage, evaluative research can feed back information which would permit a redefinition of objectives and a rechanneling of resources. Conducting such evaluation studies at strategic points in the program plan can provide a check on intermediate results and measure progress toward the long-range objective.[8]

James points out that the planning of public service programs involves three main factors: needs, resources, and attitudes.[9] For productive planning, all three of these factors have to be evaluated separately. "A public health need is a problem affecting the health of our population and which, according to prevalent cultural values, requires solution." Such needs, to be evaluated, have to be translated into administrative terms dealing with immediate and ultimate objectives. "To carry out a public health program, secondly, *resources* of trained personnel, vaccines, drugs, x-rays, special diets, clinics, etc., are required." The evaluation of available resources, both their quantity and quality, is a prerequisite to adequate planning. Finally, "effective public health programs can only rarely be conducted in the present era, unless the community attitude toward them is satisfactory." The evaluation of community attitudes involves public opinion studies designed to determine what the public knows, believes, and is willing to do or accept in regard to any specific social problem. The correct evaluation of needs, resources, and attitudes is a prerequisite for administrative program planning.

DEMONSTRATION

Given a program plan, the next step is to try it out on a demonstration basis, if possible. Quite often the demand for services and action to meet an obvious threat is so great that one cannot wait to carry out a pilot project. However, whenever possible, high priority needs to be given to the constant development of demonstration programs in order to keep up with new problems and utilize new knowledge. To be worthwhile, such demonstration programs require evaluative research. The entire rationale of a demonstration program is to test the desirability of some proposed course of action. In the absence of such a test, one learns very little from a demonstration program. As stated by Herzog, "A demonstration necessarily involves research . . . a built-in evaluation."[10] She goes on to caution, however, that while such evaluative research is essential, it should be simple "but not 'unscientific.'" The objective of a demonstration project is to demonstrate the *application* of knowledge and not to produce such knowledge.

A somewhat different attitude toward the research functions of a demonstration program is taken by James, who believes that the demonstration program offers an unusual opportunity for conducting research. He finds that the limited generalizability of demonstration projects permits a more flexible approach and the ability to experiment with new ideas involving small populations without having to adhere to the rigid requirements of a research project. He would rank systematic program development by means of demonstration projects high as a source of new ideas and practices. He cautions that "great stress should be laid upon selection of objectives, exploration of the strategic factors involved, building evaluation into the project, and retaining enough flexibility to keep the demonstration useful during its entire development. Instead of stressing only the services to be achieved, careful attention must be given in program development to the elements of failure and what can be done about them. Rather than be annoyed at the problems which arise, their appearance should be welcomed as learning opportunities."[11]

The Office of Vocational Rehabilitation sees demonstration projects as occupying a position midway between research and service. As such they have some of the characteristics of both—one learns and acquires new knowledge at the same time that one tries out new services. The Office of Vocational Rehabilitation defines the demonstration project as "the application in a practical setting of results, derived from either fundamental research or from experience in life situations, for the purpose of determining whether these knowledges or experiences are actually applicable in the practical setting chosen."[12]

Criteria for evaluating demonstration projects, as proposed by the Office of Vocational Rehabilitation, include: (1) Novelty—demonstration programs should offer something new and as yet untried. Hypotheses should be offered as to why this new approach is desirable. (2) Evaluation—systematic evaluation of the effectiveness of the demonstration must be carried out with as high standards of excellence as a basic research study. The requirements of such evaluative research involve conceptualization of the desired objectives and the development of before and after measures of the attainment of these objectives. In addition, these measures of outcomes should permit differentiation of relevant aspects rather than one overall measure and should permit the formulation of hypotheses showing the relationship between the procedures used and the behavioral outcomes.[13] (3) Generalizability—results should be practical and meaningful to normal situations and not limited to particular personnel, equipment or services. (4) Desirability—the significance and value of the project should be clear from the demonstration and its evaluation.

There is some disagreement as to whether the evaluation of a demonstration project should stress its practical or its ideal nature. On the one hand, the argument goes, "When we set out to demonstrate something we are demonstrating to ourselves and to others the relative values of meeting certain community needs in certain ways. But it goes beyond that. If our original hypotheses are proved sound, the techniques we have demonstrated should be carried on in an intensified and expanded program. 'Demonstration' connotes a limited effort with the goal of providing its validity for application on a much broader basis."[14] According to this approach, the evaluation of a demonstration program should indicate the extent to which the demonstration program is practical and can serve as a model for similar programs on a broader scale.

The opposing point of view would plan the demonstration program to stress what is ideally possible in a high quality program. Borgatta finds that "under the concept of demonstration programs, whether they be in the health services or welfare, emphasis is placed on the exemplary application of a service that is assumed already to be effective."[15] In this sense the demonstration program becomes a model program rather than a prototype for similar operating programs. This approach will often be used when there is skepticism or antagonism toward a new program and the emphasis of the evaluation is upon knowing that something worthwhile can be done, provided the required resources are made available.

Both the "typical" and the "model" demonstration programs have their own justifications. A serious error is committed, however, when an evaluation is made without taking into account the type of program and its purpose. Many operating programs prove unsuccessful despite the favorable evaluation of a demonstration project because the demonstration project was a "model" one and was conducted under more favorable circumstances than are possible for an operational program. On the other hand, while the demonstration program should attempt to reproduce conditions realistically, it is important that such conditions offer at least a reasonable possibility of success. The evaluation of a demonstration program which is weak to begin with will only prove its ineffectiveness and interfere with future opportunities for action.

Despite the obvious fact that there is little point in undertaking a demonstration program that is doomed from the start, many program directors do so anyway, probably with the mistaken notion that any demonstration program is better than none. Perhaps this is the reason that so many evaluation studies of public service and community action show negative results—the programs were never really given a fair trial. To some extent this may also explain why, as we shall see in the next section, so many program directors resist building-in evaluation to their demonstration programs. They never really had faith in the program to begin with and an evaluation could only prove embarrassing.

In evaluating a demonstration program, particular attention should be paid to the analysis of process—how and why various aspects of the program failed or succeeded, among whom the effects were most noticeable, when these effects occurred, how long they lasted, and so forth.[16] Of special importance are the possible "boomerang" or negative side effects. Detection of these in the demonstration program offers the possibility of avoiding or lessening them in the operating program. A parallel might be drawn between this aspect of program evaluation and the field trials or demonstration stage of drug research. After a new drug has been proven effective in the laboratory or clinic, it must still undergo evaluation by a field demonstration involving its use in a wide variety of actual treatment programs.

At the present time, the major emphasis of many action research projects is upon demonstration programs on the federal, state, and local levels. These demonstration programs appear to offer an acceptable compromise between research projects which are too slow and operational programs which are too experimental or expensive. The demonstration program seems to be the administrator's answer to public demand that "something be done" to meet a problem. It is quite likely, as Blum and Leonard predict:

> We predict that with motivation of public administration, many, if not most, public-service programs can and will be started as demonstrations. Quality evaluation will be built in such a way as to permit maximum flexibility. Even at what superficially seems to involve major costs, demonstrations that determine whether extensive or long-term efforts should be adopted will be the means of getting better and more extensive service at less cost than today's unevaluated, skimpy, and often ineffective programs. With improved quality of administration and scientific programming, demonstrations in one area should provide some pilot experience for others.[17]

OPERATION

A successful operational program is, of course, the ultimate goal of program planning, demonstration, and evaluation. The general purpose of program planning is to define the problem and to formulate program objectives and devise the means or activities for accomplishing these objectives. The demonstration program helps to indicate the probable success of the planned program, to try out procedures, and to suggest modifications. The evaluation provides a measure of the extent to which the demonstration or operational program attains the desired results. But it is this operational program with its actual "delivery of services" which provides the ultimate rationale for all of the other administrative processes.

Evaluative research is a basic ingredient of "scientific" program management. To the extent that operational programs are closely linked to the attainment of some desired objective rather than to the perpetuation of their own existence, they will make constant use of evaluation studies. Such evaluation studies may serve the following valuable functions for program operation.

1. Determine the extent to which program activities are achieving the desired objectives. Measure the degree of progress toward ultimate goals and indicate level of attainment.

2. Point out specific strong and weak points of program operation and suggest changes and modifications of procedures and objectives. Increase effectiveness by maximizing strengths and minimizing weaknesses.

3. Examine efficiency and adequacy of programs compared to other methods and total needs. Improve program procedures and increase scope.

4. Provide quality-controls. Set standards of performance and check on their continuous attainment.

5. Help to clarify program objectives by requiring operational definition in terms of measurable criteria. Challenge the "taken-for-granted" assumptions underlying programs. Point out inconsistencies in objectives or activities.

6. Develop new procedures and suggest new approaches and programs for future programs.

7. Provide checks on possible "boomerang" or negative side effects. Alert staff to possible changes of the program.

8. Establish priorities among programs in terms of best use of limited resources—funds, personnel, and time.

9. Indicate degree of transferability of program to other areas and populations. Suggest necessary modifications to fit changing times and places.

10. Advance scientific knowledge base of professional practice by testing effectiveness of proposed preventive and treatment programs. Suggest hypotheses for future research.

11. Advance administrative science by testing effectiveness of different organizational structures and modes of operation.

12. Provide public accountability. Justify program to public. Increase public support for successful programs and decrease demand for unnecessary or unsuccessful ones.

13. Build morale of staff by involving them in evaluation of their efforts. Provide goals and standards against which to measure progress and achievement.

14. Develop a critical attitude among staff and field personnel. Increase communication and information among program staff resulting in better coordination of services.

It must be remembered that the foregoing list is probably more applicable to the potential than the actual advantages of evaluative research. This is what evaluative research tries to accomplish; in very few instances does it actually succeed. Fleck distinguishes three types of evaluation research in relation to program operations: (1) *Ritualistic*—the development of activity indices, most often found when the goal of the program is short-term stability. "Organizational changes need not take place if the factors that produce the index are to a large extent irrelevant to the organization." (2) *Operational*—the measure of efficiency or the maximum yield per unit of cost. "The unequivocal precision obtainable by the operational method is more than offset by its failure to describe accurately the conditions under which an organization will act." (3) *Behavioral*—aimed at change to meet new conditions. Objective is long-range survival versus short-term stability. "The evaluation study revealed a great trend and provided guidelines for deliberate action."[18] It is probably true that at the present moment most evaluation studies are likely to be of the ritualistic type.

This is not too difficult to understand. Operational programs are often highly entrenched activities based upon a large collection of inadequately tested assumptions and defended by staff and field personnel with strong vested interests in the continuation of the program as it is. It is obvious from this description that an evaluation study which proposes to challenge the effectiveness of an established operational program poses a real threat to program personnel. Therefore, it is not surprising to note how rare and how difficult it is to conduct an evaluation study of an existing program. To a large extent such evaluations are limited to new programs which are still open to change. And yet the need for evaluation is undoubtedly greatest for established operating programs.

James recognizes this problem when he talks about the need "to build dissatisfaction" into traditional programs. Since it is unlikely that this dissatisfaction will come from within the program itself, he strongly suggests the use of an advisory committee of outsiders that meets regularly to review the current status of the program. This type of critical review can also be furthered through the use of interdisciplinary program teams. Given a mixture of disciplines or backgrounds, it is more likely that some member will challenge the existing program. Unless there is some dissatisfaction, James sees very little likelihood of an evaluation of an operating program. This point is underscored by Borgatta, who finds that "when conditions are bad enough and social conscience is brought into play, both the need and the potential for improvement may lead to the development of a program designed to be corrective. Most programs that receive systematic attention for evaluation occur in the context of correcting an existing situation."[19]

Change is often a stimulus to evaluating existing programs. If the state of a problem changes, or if a new method of meeting this problem is discovered, it is more likely that an attempt will be made to evaluate the desirability of continuing a traditional program. Sometimes even a change in personnel, especially at the administrative level, will provide the opportunity to reevaluate a program. A change in available resources, either in personnel or funds, may require a decision concerning the relative priority of an old or a new approach which would encourage evaluative research. Competition can be an effective stimulus toward evaluation.

It is obvious from these brief remarks that the evaluation of an ongoing, established, operational program is fraught with administrative considerations. Quite often these may lead to what we might call an "abuse" of evaluative research; that is, the evaluation is done with some other purpose than program improvement in mind. For example, we may list the following forms of evaluative "abuse" or pseudo-evaluation;

1. *Eye-wash*—an attempt to justify a weak or bad program by deliberately selecting only those aspects that "look good." The objective of the evaluation is limited to those parts of the program that appear successful.

2. *White-wash*—an attempt to cover up program failure or errors by avoiding any objective appraisal. A favorite device here is to solicit "testimonials" which divert attention from the failure.

3. *Submarine*—an attempt to "torpedo" or destroy a program regardless of its worth in order to get rid of it. This often occurs in administrative clashes over power or prestige when opponents are "sunk" along with their programs.

4. *Posture*—an attempt to use evaluation as a "gesture" of objectivity and to assume the pose of "scientific" research. This "looks good" to the public and is a sign of "professional" status.

5. *Postponement*—an attempt to delay needed action by pretending to seek the "facts." Evaluative research takes time and, hopefully, the storm will blow over by the time the study is completed.

6. *Substitution*—an attempt to "cloud over" or disguise failure in an essential part of the program by shifting attention to some less relevant, but defensible, aspect of the program.

These are only some of the many ways an ingenious administrator can utilize evaluative research to further his own rather than the program's objectives. All of these occur constantly in the "games people play" in administrative circles, but when they become systematized as "evaluation research," we feel justified in labeling them "abuses." As we shall see later in our discussion of administrator-evaluator role relationships, these misuses of evaluation pose a major ethical problem for the evaluator as researcher and may become a serious source of conflict between himself and the program staff.

Borgatta lists some of the many ways in which the results of even a well-conducted evaluation study may be rationalized so as to avoid the need to act upon negative findings.[20] These rationalizations may be used before the fact to prevent the initiation of any evaluative research, or after the fact to dismiss the findings as not significant. For example, rationalizations for avoiding evaluation include the following:

1. The effects of the program are long-range; thus, the consequences cannot be measured in the immediate future.
2. The effects are general rather than specific; thus, no single criterion can be utilized to evaluate the program, and, indeed, even using many measures would not really get at complex general consequences intended.
3. The results are small, but significant; thus, they cannot be measured effectively because instruments are not sufficiently sensitive.
4. The effects are subtle, and circumstances may not be ordered appropriately to get at the qualities that are being changed. The measurement would disturb the processes involved.
5. Experimental manipulation cannot be carried out because to withhold treatment from some persons would not be fair.

Rationalizations of negative findings, even when the evaluation study is well conducted, include:

1. The effectiveness of the program cannot really be judged because those who could use the services most did not participate.
2. Some of the persons who received the services improved greatly. Clearly, some of the persons who recovered could not have done so if they had not received attention.
3. Some of the persons who most needed the program were actually in the control group.
4. The fact that no difference was found between the persons receiving services and those not receiving services clearly indicates that the program was not sufficiently intensive. More of the services are obviously required.
5. Persons in the control group received other kinds of attention.

Occasionally one will even find the research worker being attacked because his evaluation study "failed" to find the desired effects. Thus, a "good" evaluation of a "bad" program may often be dismissed as a research failure—and not infrequently, the evaluator will apologize for his lack of positive findings.

A major effort to place the evaluation of operational programs on a "scientific" basis and to decrease the possibilities of bias or abuse is represented by the rapidly growing field of operations research. Using a systematic and comprehensive approach which involves all four processes of program planning, demonstration, operation, and evaluation, operations research attempts to develop models of interaction, often utilizing mathematical concepts, which provide guidelines for the most productive and efficient use of available resources to meet specified objectives. This method is highly technical and requires detailed treatment in its own right. Several excellent books deal with the theory and practice of this approach.[21]

In general, operations research consists of the following steps:

This approach has been used quite successfully in relation to hospital operation and other health services.[22] As described by James, "Operations research has helped greatly to clear the air for public health evaluation by stressing and not glossing over the compromises between research findings and the art of public health practice. If it should reveal, for example, that restaurant sanitation emphasizes goals that are aesthetic rather than disease-preventing, then attention can be switched to technics which can achieve a maximum aesthetic return for the least effort."[23]

An important aspect of evaluation in relation to operations research is the continuous check it provides upon determining the optimal combination of program practices related to the desired goal. By stating the conditions under which certain procedures will attain predetermined goals, operations research provides for the "establishment of evaluation machinery with an apparatus for new decision-making when the key variables change beyond predetermined limits."[24] Evaluation is thus an essential feature of all aspects of operations research.

One component of evaluative research that is often neglected and that constitutes an important aspect of operations research is the cost of a program. Few programs can be justified at any cost. Priorities among public services must often be determined on the basis of the most desirable allocation of resources—money, personnel, facilities. Competition among service programs sets the stage for a public demand for evaluation of results in terms of required resources. Weisbrod points out that while improved health is desirable, so are improved housing, highways, flood control, recreation facilities, and so on. Since we cannot have everything, we must economize. He concludes, "To make choices in a rational manner requires estimation of the relative importance of the various alternatives. . . . With this general possibility in mind, increasing attention has come to be paid to estimating in money terms the real importance of good health—or, what is the same thing, estimating losses from poor health. . . ."[25]

Arbona stresses the importance of evaluating the positive effects of action programs in a nation's economy. "It is very important to design a methodology that will demonstrate to the satisfaction of all, but especially of the economists, how investments in health result in the improvement of a nation's economy. This need is especially vital in developing countries where resources are limited and other services generally absorb so large a proportion of national budgets that health services' support is meager compared to needs."[26] The development of program and performance budgeting for public service programs represents an attempt to introduce the "cost" criterion into evaluative research.[27,28] In using these cost criteria, however, one must keep in mind the social aspects of such a financial evaluation. As Flagle cautions, "The construction of a table or scale of utilities, although cast in terms of economics, is essentially a psychological experiment involving social values."[29]

RESISTANCE AND BARRIERS TO EVALUATION

Few individuals with strongly vested interests in the programs they are conducting can be expected to welcome an objective evaluation. Many of them have been "socialized" into taking the worthwhileness of their activities for granted and are naturally resistant to having these activities and their underlying assumptions challenged.[30] Furthermore, many of them are sincerely convinced that evaluative research is not really "scientific" and cannot be relied upon to produce reliable and valid results. Others are too caught up in the daily demands of providing "obviously necessary" services to take the time for research, especially if this requires an interruption or modification of services or the reallocation of limited resources.

A good example of such administrative resistance is offered by Wright and Hyman in describing their experiences in evaluating the Encampment for Citizenship.

> . . . There is reason for the researcher to be apprehensive about such matters. The staff of such institutions as the Encampment often have invested considerable time, effort, and sentiment in their programs. They may be ego-involved in their activities. They may be sensitive to the cold-blooded, objective probings of the scientific researcher. Even under favorable circumstances, it is common to find that action-oriented and dedicated persons are unreceptive to social science. . . . How much more likely a hostile reaction may be if such measurements threaten to reveal unfavorable information![31]

The literature on evaluative research contains some examples of evaluation studies which have produced "negative" results. Yankauer and his colleagues discuss the doubtful benefits of annual school physical examinations;[32] Wilner and his associates after a careful evaluation of housing projects point out the minor health advantages of such projects despite optimistic claims to the contrary;[33] Meyer and Borgatta could find very little positive impact in a well-planned rehabilitation program for mental patients.[34] And, as James points out, for each of these tested programs there are dozens of untested programs which continue in existence despite any convincing evidence of their accomplishments.[35]

Administrative resistance is also likely to be magnified if there is the possibility of a conflict between the goals or objectives of the program and the goals or objectives of the organization itself. Organizations and administrative structures will tend to perpetuate themselves. The organizational goals thus become those of survival, stability, power, and growth. These may conflict with the program goals of the organization, which may be to do away with a problem—and hence the need for the organization. If the results of the evaluation study tend to weaken the power of the organization, such a study will tend to be resisted. Even if the study is conducted and the results indicate that the organization has done such a good job that it is in danger of putting itself out of business, organizational pressures will tend to seek a new problem area to justify the continuation of the organization. The proposition as stated by Berelson and Steiner reads, "There is a tendency for organizations to equate power with purpose, or even to place power above purpose, so that survival as an organization becomes an end in itself. . . . An oversimplified way to put this is to say that most organizations will adjust rather than die: after all, they are made up of human beings who will do the same."[36]

NOTES TO CHAPTER VIII

1. Lewis, C. I., "An Analysis of Knowledge and Valuation," *The Paul Carus Foundation Lectures VII.* The Open Court Publishing Co., La Salle, Ill., 1946, p. 3.
2. Knutson, Andie L., "Evaluating Health Education," *Public Health Reports,* vol. 67, January, 1952, pp. 73–77.
3. James, George, "Research by Local Health Departments—Problems, Methods, Results," *American Journal of Public Health,* vol. 48, March, 1958, p. 354.
4. James, George, "Planning and Evaluation of Health Programs," in *Administration of Community Health Services.* International City Managers' Association, Chicago, 1961, chap. 6.
5. Gouldner, Alvin W., "Theoretical Requirements of the Applied Social Sciences," *American Sociological Review,* vol. 22, February, 1957, pp. 92–102.
6. Merton, Robert K., "The Role of Applied Social Science in the Formation of Policy," *Philosophy of Science,* vol. 16, July, 1949, pp. 161–181.
7. Blood, J. W., editor, *PERT: A New Management Planning and Control Technique.* American Management Association, New York, 1962.
8. "Evaluation in Public Health," *Public Health Reports,* vol. 71, June, 1956, pp. 526–527.
9. James, George, "The Present Status and Future Development of Community Health Research—A Critique from the Viewpoint of Community Health Agencies," *Annals of the New York Academy of Sciences,* vol. 107, May 22, 1963, p. 761.
10. Herzog, Elizabeth, "Research Demonstrations and Common Sense," *Child Welfare,* June, 1962, p. 245.
11. James, George, "Planning and Evaluation of Health Programs," *op. cit.,* p. 133.
12. Criswell, John W., *The Place of Demonstration Projects in the Program of the Office of Vocational Rehabilitation.* Washington, August, 1962, p. 1. Mimeographed.
13. *Ibid.,* p. 2.
14. *Planning Evaluations of Mental Health Programs.* Milbank Memorial Fund, New York, 1958, p. 49.
15. Borgatta, Edgar F., "Research Problems in Evaluation of Health Service Demonstrations," *Milbank Memorial Fund Quarterly,* vol. 44, part 2, October, 1966, p. 196.
16. As stressed by Blum and Leonard, "If the demonstration ultimately proves successful and accomplishes its objectives, the key to its adoption or usefulness elsewhere may be not so much in the proof of effectiveness as in knowledge of the steps that resulted in its development and secured participation and acceptance." Blum, Hendrik L., and Alvin R. Leonard,

Public Administration: A Public Health Viewpoint, Macmillan Co., New York, 1963, p. 318.

17. *Ibid.,* p. 320.
18. Fleck, Andrew C., "Evaluation Research Programs in Public Health Practice," *Annals of the New York Academy of Sciences,* vol. 107, May 22, 1963, pp. 721–723.
19. Borgatta, Edgar F., *op. cit.,* pp. 183–184. To some extent, the conditions specified by Merton and Devereux for creating public concern about a social problem also promote evaluative research: "(1) A *perceived discrepancy* between some existing (or future) external situation, on the one hand, and the values or goals of an individual or organization, on the other; (2) A feeling of a *need for adjustive activity* or for creative action of some sort; (3) A 'puzzle element'—an *awareness of ignorance or doubt* about at least some of the facts and relationships believed to be relevant to a decision about what, if anything, should be done." Merton, Robert K., and Edward C. Devereux, Jr., "Practical Problems and the Uses of Social Science," *Transaction,* July, 1964, pp. 18–21.
20. Borgatta, Edgar F., *ibid.,* pp. 186–187.
21. McCloskey, Joseph F., and Florence N. Trefethen, editors, *Operations Research for Management.* Johns Hopkins Press, Baltimore, 1954; Churchman, C. West, Russell L. Ackoff, and E. Leonard Arnoff, *Introduction to Operations Research,* John Wiley and Sons, New York, 1957.
22. Flagle, Charles D., "Operational Research in the Health Services," *Annals of the New York Academy of Sciences,* vol. 107, May 22, 1963, pp. 748–759; Feldstein, Martin S., "Operational Research and Efficiency in Health Service," *The Lancet,* March, 1963, pp. 491–493.
23. James, George, "Research by Local Health Departments—Problems, Methods, Results," *op. cit.,* p. 355.
24. Anderson, Otis L., "Operations Research in Public Health," *Public Health Reports,* vol. 79, April, 1964, pp. 297–305.
25. Weisbrod, Burton A., "Does Better Health Pay?" *Public Health Reports,* vol. 75, June, 1960, p. 557.
26. Arbona, Guillermo, "Public Health Progress in Puerto Rico," *Public Health Reports,* vol. 79, January, 1964, p. 42.
27. Taubenhaus, L. J., R. H. Hamlin, and R. C. Wood, "Performance Reporting and Program Budgeting: Tools for Program Evaluation," *American Journal of Public Health,* vol. 47, April, 1957, pp. 432–438.
28. James, George, Daniel Klepak, and Herman E. Hilleboe, "Fiscal Research in Public Health," *American Journal of Public Health,* vol. 45, July, 1955, pp. 906–914.
29. Flagle, Charles D., *op. cit.,* p. 758.
30. Such resistance to changes in established values and practices extends beyond the administrator to the community itself. This has been substantiated by many studies of attempts to change community programs. For example, as described by Lewis: "Those who enter a community to engage in an action program must recognize the implications of the fact that they are not entering a power vacuum. In every human community there

exists a network of relations between individuals. It is to the interest of
many of these individuals to maintain this system of relationships. Any
group of outsiders moving into a community will be seen by some as potentially disruptive, even if they plan no action. If they do plan action,
whatever positive measures they undertake, no matter how benign, will
be perceived by some community members as a threat to their own status
and interests." Lewis, Oscar, "Medicine and Politics in a Mexican Vil-
lage," in Paul, Benjamin D., editor, *Health, Culture, and Community.*
Russell Sage Foundation, New York, 1955, p. 431.
31. Wright, Charles R., and Herbert H. Hyman, "The Evaluators," in Hammond, Phillip E., editor, *Sociologists at Work.* Basic Books, New York,
1964, p. 123.
32. Yankauer, A., and others, "A Study of Periodic School Medical Examinations," *American Journal of Public Health,* vol. 45, January, 1955, pp. 71–
78; vol. 46, December, 1956, pp. 1553–1562; vol. 47, November, 1957,
pp. 1421–1429; vol. 52, April, 1962, pp. 656–657.
33. Wilner, Daniel M., R. P. Walkley, T. C. Pinkerton, and M. Tayback,
Housing Environment and Family Life. Johns Hopkins Press, Baltimore,
1962.
34. Meyer, Henry J., and Edgar F. Borgatta, *An Experiment in Mental Patient Rehabilitation.* Russell Sage Foundation, New York, 1959.
35. James, George, "Research by Local Health Departments—Problems,
Methods, Results," *op. cit.* Specifically, he points out, "One of the sim-
plest methods of doing this is to carry out a survey to collect relevant data
concerning needs, resources and attitudes, carry out the program, and
then to repeat the survey to evaluate the changes. Curiously enough, although steps one and two are fairly common, health officers have done
relatively little with step three. By the time step three is reached, the
program is deemed a success and evaluation relegated to a low priority.
This has been the case with both child guidance and crippled children's
programs, two amazing instances of the lack of priority given to the
follow-up of the hundreds of thousands who have received such care in
every section of the country during the past two decades." (p. 356)
36. Berelson, Bernard, and Gary Steiner, *Human Behavior: An Inventory of
Scientific Findings.* Harcourt, Brace and World, Inc., New York, 1964.
A good example of this process may be seen in the National Foundation
which shifted its goals from poliomyelitis to children's disabilities in general after the former problem had been brought under control. MacIntosh
goes so far as to claim that the major objective of many voluntary agencies
which are focused upon some specific social problem should be aimed at
"self-extinction." From a talk before the Eastern States Health Conference on "Voluntary Action in the British Health Services," New York,
April 27, 1961.

CHAPTER IX

The Administration of Evaluation Studies

So far we have been concerned mainly with the ways in which evaluative research relates to the administrative process—what we have called evaluation *in* administration. We now turn our attention to those administrative factors which affect the objectives, design, execution, and utilization of evaluation studies—or the administration *of* evaluative research.

To begin with, it is important to note that research itself requires administration. A research project is a form of social activity encompassing a number of highly significant interpersonal relationships between and among research workers, program personnel, and subjects. As Sjoberg has maintained, science itself has strong normative overtones.[1] The methods employed represent "acceptable and appropriate" deviations from the canons of the scientific method and are usually a compromise between the ideal and the practical. As we noted elsewhere, research can rarely be conducted under ideal conditions and all research projects, even those in the physical sciences, represent a combination of scientific and administrative considerations.[2]

Nowhere is this more true than in evaluative research. In addition to the general normative aspects of basic research, the evaluator deals with objectives and hypotheses that are closely tied to vested interests. He is not the objective scholar in search of new knowledge so much as the judge of success or failure. He may sincerely believe that this judgment can best be made by use of the tools of the objective scholar; however, in the final analysis, his conclusions do not represent the acceptance or rejection of a neutral hypothesis but recommendations which may affect the continuation or change of a program. His results reach a world beyond that of his fellow scientists—a world of program personnel and recipients of service. As such, his research is subject to social constraints from both the organization within which he is working and the larger society which requires the services of this organization.

These constraints, as we shall see, set limits on many different aspects of the evaluative research project. This chapter will discuss briefly the following problems in the administration of evaluative research:

1. Relation to public demand and cooperation
2. Resources for evaluative research
3. Role relationships and value conflicts
4. Definition of evaluation problem and objectives
5. Evaluative research design and execution
6. Utilization of findings

Each of these problems is more or less present in any social research project. By and large, however, these problems are less dominant and tend to be overlooked in nonevaluative studies. To some degree they also explain why many social research workers are reluctant to take part in evaluative research projects. But, as we will argue in the final chapter, such projects provide both a challenge and an opportunity to social research to advance theory and knowledge concerning social action and change and to offer the possibility for "social experimentation" under natural field conditions.

RELATION TO PUBLIC DEMAND AND COOPERATION

To an increasing extent, the public is taking an active role in determining what services it will receive. Partly, this is the result of an increased need to secure public participation and partly, it represents the absence of professional guidelines which would enable the public service administrator to know what services would be best for the public. The current accent of the War on Poverty on "self-help" programs places a premium on the community's own definition of its needs for service.

While in some cases the public demand will be for evaluation and proof of the effectiveness of programs, for the most part the emphasis will be upon the immediate delivery of services. Thus, "popular causes" spring up which bring pressure upon the program administrator to satisfy public demand regardless of professional judgment or evaluation findings. As described by James, "Many a health officer will say, 'It does not matter what I prove, the community will still insist upon the same extensive school health, restaurant sanitation, or milk control programs. The citizens have become conditioned to them. They believe them necessary and no glib, small research project is going to change their minds.' "[3] The difficulty experienced by many communities in securing fluoridation despite evaluation study after evaluation study attesting to its effectiveness, underscores this relationship of evaluative research to public opinion.[4]

Another aspect of evaluative research affected by public demand concerns the resistance of the public to withholding services until the completion of evaluation studies. Once sufficient evidence has accumulated to indicate the potential benefits of a program, the public is likely to demand the program without waiting for conclusive proof. The greater the need, the stronger the pressure to put the program into operation as soon as it begins to look successful. While clinical medicine has to some extent been able to resist such pressures by its traditional insistence upon controlled studies of new drugs or treatments, social service programs in welfare, education, and public health have not been so successful.

Finally, brief mention should be made of the dependence of much programmatic evaluative research upon the voluntary cooperation of the public as subjects. The public cannot be ordered to participate in an evaluation study and, indeed, may actively resent the intrusion of such research upon its privacy or freedom of choice. If the study is limited to volunteers, as it often must be, then the researcher faces serious problems of bias through the self-selective nature of his sample. An additional ethical problem is introduced when a random assignment of voluntary subjects must be made to experimental and control groups. Withholding treatment or services from a control group that wants or needs such services is likely to create both public relations and methodological problems for the evaluator. On the other hand, giving treatment or services of unknown value with the possibility of negative side effects to the experimental group raises problems of using the public as "guinea pigs." It is doubtful that any research technique can be developed to take care of these problems—they are inherent in all natural field experimentation.

RESOURCES FOR EVALUATIVE RESEARCH

Evaluation, like all research, requires money, time, facilities, and, perhaps most of all, trained personnel. As we have stated previously, evaluative research is first and foremost research and it is doubtful that such research can be carried out successfully by someone who does not have the knowledge and skills of a research worker. In fact, the methodological difficulties of evaluative research demand better-trained rather than less well-trained research workers, as is often assumed. Many, if not most, evaluation studies are undertaken by service personnel completely lacking in a knowledge of research design or techniques for the collection and analysis of data.

We must grant, however, that this is often a case of necessity; there simply are not enough research personnel available for evaluation studies. But to some extent this condition reflects the low priority given to evaluation compared with services when it comes to allocating funds and personnel. Literally billions of dollars will be spent for service programs without any serious attempt to determine whether these programs are accomplishing anything worthwhile. This is especially noticeable in relation to the current War on Poverty where lip service rather than hard cash is being given to the need for evaluative research.

In general, evaluation studies cannot simply be "tacked on" to existing service programs making use of untrained service personnel to do the research. Such research is likely to prove valueless or, even worse, misleading. It is questionable whether these "amateur" evaluation studies should be encouraged. If one looks for other benefits besides objective evaluation, there are certain advantages that do accrue to self-evaluations. As stated by Blum and Leonard:

> In general, the staff secure new concepts and become much more knowledgeable in the area of the research. They often learn new approaches and techniques that become useful in their daily work. If it is a well-run project, they develop a kind of critical discernment that comes from setting up hypotheses and avoiding conflicting or confusing methods and approaches. They learn to look for erroneous analogies, inadequate hypotheses, and poor design, methodology, and evaluation. They may not learn enough to be able to design good projects themselves, but they become more aware of the good and bad proposals which are presented to them as part of the operating programs.[5]

On the other hand, these same authors point out:

> The possibility of confusing research objectives with those of daily work cannot be eliminated, particularly if the work involves education or interviewing, such as public health nurses do. Careful indoctrination as part of good research methodology should leave very little of an experimental design open to the chance influence of daily work. However, where especially concise approaches or denial of supposedly beneficial services to control groups of clients is contemplated, the service-oriented staff may emotionally be unable to comply. In addition, conflict of emergency duties with research obligations will usually find the research work put aside while clients' needs are being met. This can result in costly deferment or neglect.[6]

Until evaluative research attains more of the prestige and recognition of nonevaluative research, it is probable that most evaluation studies will

continue to be carried out by service personnel with mixed advantages
and disadvantages.

To a large extent, the role relationships and conflicts between an administrator and an evaluator are the same as those that have been discussed
in some detail for the administrator and researcher in any applied or service program setting. A survey by Russell Sage Foundation of 65 social
scientists engaged in Foundation-supported projects in various applied
settings classified the causes of collaborative conflict into three major
categories:

1. Differing cultural backgrounds which affect languages, values,
   goals, and perceptions;
2. Low-status work within a rigid, status-conscious institutional setting;
3. Differing conceptions of self and expectations of others.[7]

This same study concluded that these researcher-practitioner conflicts
are not easy to overcome; they require a very substantial expenditure of
time and energy on both sides even when the parties to the undertaking
appear eager to collaborate fully. As helpful moves in this direction, the
following were suggested:

1. Developing an optimal initial orientation and level of expectation
   on the part of both the social scientist [*read evaluator*] and the
   public health practitioner.
2. Maximizing mutual assimilation of professional subcultural values, ideologies, technologies, and language.
3. Securing an appropriate structural position in the institutional setting for the social scientist. He must be given the usual preroga-
   tives of autonomy in his research with full access to policy-makers.
4. Clarification of the roles of the parties to the undertaking. The
   social scientist must accept responsibility for developing the
   proper role of social scientist and not pseudo-practitioner.
5. Increasing the interpersonal skills of the participants. While personal qualities, skills, and modes of responding are important,
   "personality clashes" all too frequently are offered as explanations
   for difficulties which could be more accurately perceived and
   more efficiently dealt with as cultural, social-structural, and role-
   specification problems.

Evaluative research is even more likely than nonevaluative research to
put a strain upon the working relationships between the evaluator and

the administrator and staff of the operating program. After all, the primary function of the evaluator is to determine whether or not a program is attaining its desired objectives and this cannot help but pose a threat to the staff and create apprehension on the part of the evaluator. Wright and Hyman accent the following questions: Were the sponsors aware of what they were undertaking? Would they permit the researcher the necessary freedom of inquiry? How would they react to negative findings?[8]

We have already noted some of the forms of resistance to evaluative research which personnel present. The resistance is often translated into open conflict between the service worker and the evaluator in the course of the evaluation project. Quite often the evaluation has been requested by some outside agency or by the central office and the field personnel are likely to feel that they are on trial. The program staff may believe that no problem exists and that the evaluation is an interference with their activities and a waste of time. Many may be skeptical about the scientific validity of the evaluation study or about the subsequent application of its results. The demands of the research design, especially insofar as they require the withholding of services, might run contrary to the professional standards of the service personnel. Furthermore, the practitioner is largely "here and now" oriented with strong pressures for the immediate delivery of services, while the evaluator is more likely to be concerned with long-term goals. These barriers to collaboration between evaluator and practitioner constitute serious obstacles to the successful conduct of evaluative research.

Bergen makes this point in his review of evaluation projects in the field of community mental health. His major charge is that the results of evaluative research are largely inadequate because "the requisites for systematic research, which are often obvious enough, meet inordinate difficulties in being accepted and carried out. There often seems to be, for lack of a better term, a 'defensiveness' associated with carrying them through. . . . This, we suggest, is rooted in the need to integrate, in order to accomplish this evaluation, practice and research in a common endeavor."[9]

The problem of integrating or coordinating evaluator and practitioner has given rise to the usual assortment of admonitions concerning the need for mutual understanding and respect. Thus, the evaluator and program personnel are advised to sit down together before the evaluation takes place to discuss the objectives and plan of procedure. They are told that collaboration is a two-way street and that each must try to learn the other's language so that they can communicate, and that, while they have different disciplinary orientations, these need not interfere with their ability to get along. As Herzog points out, much of this discussion resembles that of someone describing and urging "love." But she goes on, "interdisciplinary research, unlike love, has standard early phases that are usually wasteful and often painful, and that seem avoidable to those who have lived through them. Yet these efforts, on the whole, seem more successful in producing hearty agreement from those who have lived through them than in forestalling interdisciplinary pains for those who have not."[10]

A practical suggestion is offered by Metzner and Gurin, who stress the desirability for the evaluation team to be "useful" to the program team by offering both help and suggestions. However, they caution: "To the extent that this involves uncritical acceptance of the aims and explanations of the group whose work is being studied, and absorbs a great amount of the available time, it is detrimental to the evaluation. The aim, therefore, must be to maintain a position of friendly detachment and entails constant dangers of over-involvement or rejection, and requires variation and reassessment as the work goes on."[11]

On a more operational level, a major decision in evaluative research concerns the use of an "outside" evaluator versus someone, even a professional research worker, already connected with the program. The question, "Who should do the evaluation?" is not answerable in any clear-cut way, since both internal and external evaluations have advantages and disadvantages of their own. The arguments for using an outside evaluator include those of increased objectivity and the ability to see things which persons connected with the program might simply take for granted. The outside evaluator has less ego-involvement in the outcome of the evaluation and will feel less pressure to make compromises in the research design or the interpretation of the results. On the other hand, he is less likely to understand the objectives or procedures of the program and to be less sensitive to either the possible disruptions of the evaluation study to service or the practicality of the recommendations which stem from the research. As an outsider he also represents a threat to the program staff and has to face the many forms of resistance discussed previously.[12]

Evaluation by someone connected with the operating program has counter advantages and disadvantages. On the positive side, an inside evaluator is more informed about the program and is in a better position to know which aspects require evaluation. He is also more readily accepted by the program staff, especially if the staff view the study as a self-evaluation for their own good. Such a self-evaluation is also more likely to result in an application of the results of the study toward program improvement. On the negative side, it is extremely difficult for an insider in a self-evaluation to maintain objectivity. There is an almost irresistible tendency to focus upon the successful aspects of the program and to overlook the "minor" weaknesses or failures. Certain procedures which have a time-honored validity will rarely be brought into question. From a technical point of view it is also much less likely that the program staff will possess the required research knowledge and skills to conduct a professional evaluation study.

It is probable that the answer to inside versus outside evaluation will depend largely upon particular circumstances. Whenever possible, however, a combination of both has many advantages in a kind of division of labor. The inside group plays a major role in defining and formulating the objectives of the program and the activities to be evaluated—in consultation with the outside evaluator who is encouraged to raise questions. The outside group then designs the evaluation study, also in cooperation with the inside group, and tries to set it up in such a way as to interfere with normal procedures as little as possible. The actual evaluation is then carried out by both groups joining in the collection of the required data. The outside group assumes the major role in analyzing the data and presenting the results of the evaluation. Finally, these results are translated into recommendations for program changes by the inside group which continues to have the responsibility for implementation.[13]

DEFINITION OF EVALUATION PROBLEMS AND OBJECTIVES

As we have indicated, the statement of an evaluative hypothesis is a basic step in the evaluation process. This hypothesis should take the form of relating specified program activities to the desired objectives. The definition of these objectives, especially the operational criteria by which their attainment will be judged, and the specification of those activities which are designed to achieve these objectives constitute major administrative problems for evaluative research.

Part of the difficulty in defining objectives springs from the different value positions of the evaluator and the administrator or program staff as discussed above. In general, the evaluator will seek to measure achievement, while the program personnel will be more likely to emphasize effort or technique. The evaluator will be more concerned with higher level or ultimate objectives, while the practitioner will be more involved with lower-level or immediate objectives. To the evaluator, the criteria of success will deal more directly with improvement in the status of the recipients of services, while for the staff, the tendency will be to seek criteria which reflect the smoothness and efficiency of the services themselves rather than their effect upon the people to whom the services are provided.

Quite often the evaluator will be called in to evaluate a program only to find that the objectives of this program, much less its criteria of success, have never been clearly defined. What is more serious, he may find that there are wide differences of opinion among practitioners as to what they are trying to accomplish.

For example, it is still undoubtedly true, as Katinsky and Witmer had occasion to remark in 1955, that the field of community health lacks a high degree of "coherence" and organization. A notable lack of clarity and often sharply conflicting views exist about such fundamental matters as the meaning of "preventing" mental illness, the appropriate conditions for practicing different methods of treatment and care of patients, and, not least of all, what the community itself can offer and how it can be used successfully in programs directed toward these ends.[14]

Given this lack of coherence about objectives, it is little wonder that, as MacMahon and his colleagues have pointed out, efforts to evaluate the accomplishments of community mental health programs are "conspicuous by their absence."[15] They also criticize the tendency of evaluation studies in general to concentrate upon an "evaluation of technique." These require no clear-cut statement of objectives and can be limited to a measure of the quality of whatever work is done.

Another potential area of misunderstanding and conflict between the evaluator and the administrator concerns the scientific versus practical objectives of an evaluation study. The administrator is understandably concerned about the utility of the findings for improving his program, while the evaluator may knowingly or unknowingly be inclined to stress the more lasting contribution of the study to knowledge. One may be seeking involvement and help, while the other tries to avoid involvement and sticks to facts. The answer, as in the case of the previous conflicts mentioned, once again must be found in some acceptable compromise. As suggested by a World Health Organization report on evaluation, "Evaluation is intended to aid, not hamper, a project. It will serve no good purpose if those who work in a project become so preoccupied with the search for precise measurements of value that little is done to produce value. Such preoccupation is no more desirable than the other extreme, i.e., when the purpose or goal of a project is submerged and lost in the absorbing or distracting details of its day-to-day technical operation. In the one case, the project seems to exist for the sake of measurement; in the other, value is taken for granted and effort is interpreted as progress."[16]

In regard to differences in the value framework of the policy-maker as compared to that of the evaluative research worker, Merton points out that certain "value constants" are always present in applied research which "circumscribe the alternative lines of action to be investigated" and "at once limit the range and type of research which will be done with his support."[17] The value framework of the evaluator as a research worker, on the other hand, often requires him to challenge the basic assumptions of the program operator and to follow the implications of his data into areas of possible change which may appear inadvisable to the administrator.

The potentialities of a value conflict between evaluator and administrator are greatest when "why" questions are asked—"Is this really so?" and "Can you prove it?" as compared to "how" questions—"How many cases exist?" and "How can this be done?" The former questions challenge basic assumptions, while the latter pertain only to techniques or procedures. Cumming gives the following interesting example of an evaluation which succeeded in asking a "why" question:

> Mental health movements over the last ten years have given a lot of attention, for instance, to the supposed fact that employers are unhappy about taking on people who have been in mental hospitals. . . . So we say there is an undeserved stigma associated with mental illness and we have to educate employers so that they will not discriminate against patients.
>
> However, Simon Olshansky, a researcher, said to himself, "Is it really so?" He studied a population of patients discharged from the State Hospitals in the Boston vicinity. He eliminated from the group those who might suffer discrimination on other grounds, such as age or ethnicity. For the balance, he found that those who had good job histories before going into the hospital had good job histories after coming out of the hospital and those who had failed before failed afterwards. We must now take a new view of this problem.[18]

Whether or not one conducts a "why" or a "how" evaluation will depend to a large extent upon the statement of one's objectives. "Goal-setting" is the first and probably the most crucial stage of the evaluation process.

This problem has already been discussed in some detail in Chapters III and IV.

As we have indicated in the chapters on the methodology of evaluative research, evaluation, like all research, must rest upon the logic of the scientific method and make use of whatever research techniques are available and feasible. We have taken the position that research is a social enterprise representing the currently existing norms of practicing scientists and attempts to find the best possible compromise between the demands of science and the realistic conditions of research. In an interesting paper on the research process Clausen talks about "reality testing" in research, by which he means the constant checking of one's research problem and design against the *realities* of data collection and analysis. He states, "In many programs, however, decisions have to be made at least partly in terms of administrative pressures. If this is so, and if one wishes to conduct research which gives the basis for inferences about decision-making, a concern with administrative policy and administrative pressures must be built into the research design."[19]

In the present section, we will not attempt to review the many administrative problems in evaluative research discussed in the previous chapters on methodology. As we have seen in regard to the definition of objectives, administrative forces are felt at the very beginning of the project in terms of the statement of objectives and the specification of activities to be evaluated. They continue to be felt in the laying out of the research design, in selecting the sample, in the collection of the data, and in the analysis and interpretation of the results. There is no way to avoid such administrative "interferences" with the evaluative research study. Evaluation research is applied research; it has to take place in the field under natural conditions and it has to adapt itself as best it can to the practical conditions of programmatic research.

But this does not and should not mean the complete abandonment of scientific controls. If anything, it calls for an even greater awareness of the need for these controls and an ingenuity and alertness on the part of the research worker toward assuring their presence to the greatest degree possible. The problems being studied are real-life problems and the services offered as solutions to these problems represent a complex array of programs and services involving the activities of a wide range of professional and nonprofessional personnel. To make sense, these problems must be studied as they exist in the real world and the services must be evaluated under realistic administrative conditions. It does little good to remove these problems and services to the "laboratory" where they can be studied under more controlled conditions if, in so doing, one destroys the very essence of their reality. Rather than adapt the problems to fit existing methods and techniques, one must adapt the existing methods and techniques to fit the problem. In short, as Meyer and Borgatta point out, one must do one's best and push for perfection as hard as one can but accept compromise where necessary. However, they caution, "it is of no help to the orderly development of scientific knowledge to accept these studies as demonstrations of success or failure when it is possible to attempt more rigorous research. The state of our ignorance and the means of overcoming it should be accepted so that we may proceed slowly, and often painfully, to gain secure knowledge of what is being accomplished."[20]

UTILIZATION OF FINDINGS

A much debated but still unresolved question in social research is the extent to which a research worker should "go beyond his data" in making recommendations for action. One side believes that such a role will interfere with the researcher's scientific objectivity, while the other side feels that the researcher is probably in the best position to know the implications of his findings and that, by making it quite clear that he is making recommendations and not presenting results, he can separate his role as researcher from that of action adviser.[21]

While this debate may have a certain legitimacy in regard to nonevaluative research, it seems to us academic when it comes to evaluation studies. The results of the evaluation study to have any meaning at all must be translated into judgments concerning program success or failure. The more specific the evaluation is in terms of program components and service activities and the more analytical it is of the process of why these activities failed or succeeded in attaining their objectives, the more unavoidable is a discussion of possible changes to correct deficiencies in the program.

Such recommendations will benefit greatly from consultation with the administrator and program staff, in terms of both practicality and future implementation. The more involved the service personnel can become in interpreting the results of the evaluation and in formulating the recommendations, the more acceptable are these likely to be and the greater chance they will have of being put into practice. Probably one of the most serious errors an evaluator can make is to draw up a list of suggested program changes without discussing these beforehand with the personnel most affected. This does not mean that the personnel must like the proposed changes, only that they must understand the basis on which these changes are being made.

The importance of staff understanding and acceptance of the findings of an evaluation study as a prelude to change are underscored by Dressel and Mayhew in their discussion of educational evaluation. They point out that, "The role of evaluation in general education is likely to be whatever teachers and administrators assign to it. Even in cases where much in the way of evaluation has been done, there may be little apparent effect in the general education program unless the results are understood and accepted by the faculty."[22]

As mentioned previously, Merton analyzes some of the major reasons that applied research such as an evaluation study may fail to influence policy or practice. He divides these into "scientific gaps" which deal with the inability of the research findings to take into account the many contingencies of practical action and the "interpersonal and organizational gaps" which create problems of implementation based upon nonresearch considerations such as the attitude of the policy-maker toward change.[23]

There can be little doubt that most administrators expect evaluative research to be "useful." In fact, one of the major sources of reluctance to support evaluative research is a skepticism about the practical value of such research. And yet most practitioners are strongly aware of the need to assess how well they are performing their jobs and what they are accomplishing—even though they may approach the prospect with trepidation. This point has also been noted by Dressel and Mayhew:

> The instructor is concerned with instruction, and evaluation must make a direct contribution to this if it is to be of interest to him. . . . He realizes that because objectives are not clear, they have commonly played little part in the selection of course materials and experiences which are likely, therefore, to have been selected on the grounds of personal judgment as to their intrinsic worth. Similarly, his techniques of instruction are commonly highly traditional and bear little relation to the desired outcomes. His hope is that evaluation can become the means for drawing together into an integrated whole these elements of the curriculum which too often are fortuitously determined rather than systematically planned.[24]

The major factors which affect the utilization of evaluative research findings may be divided into those which relate to the program and its organization and those which deal with the public reaction to change.

1. *Related to Program and Organizational Forces.* As we have pointed out, organizations and program staff tend to resist change especially where such change challenges either the continued existence of the organization or staff or the basic assumptions underlying their objectives or procedures. Traditional activities and entrenched power are not willingly surrendered. As one public health administrator described it, the problem of discarding old programs is reminiscent of the Australian farmer who bought a new set of boomerangs and drove himself crazy trying to throw the old ones away.

Probably the most effective way to deal with organizations and staff pressures is to make these active forces in the reorganization of a program. The possibility of redirection of a program into more productive channels based upon the results of an evaluation study can be presented as a challenge to the existing staff. The more such redirection can build upon current activities involving a gradual change-over to new approaches, the more likely is it to be accepted and promoted by the staff itself.

The results of the evaluation study must be viewed as only one aspect of the problem of program change. Administrative decision-making needs to balance these results against many other factors in proposing the reorganization of a program or the reassignment of personnel. If this point is made clear to administrator and staff, then the evaluation study may not assume the exaggerated importance often attached to it, and it will tend to be accepted as only one more helpful source of information for decision-making.

An additional approach which will make the recommendations of an evaluation study more useful is to translate these recommendations into the actual organizational or procedural changes that might be developed to implement the recommendations. Too often, evaluation studies offer only broad generalizations about why programs are not succeeding, without attempting either to make these reasons more specific or to suggest what might be done about them.

This problem is raised directly by a state health commissioner: "Possibly social science should broaden its competence to make it more useful to a health agency. . . . How much better off is he (the health administrator) now, to know that the reasons for their (the people's) unfavorable reaction lie in a centuries-old tradition which has little relation to modern living? He probably suspected that anyway."[25] And it is echoed by a city health commissioner: "It is essential to recognize and work through the mores and cultural patterns. . . . But if this is as fundamental a social science principle as I think it is, how can we bring it to bear on some of the operating problems of New York City? We know, for example, that the infant mortality rate in such subcultures within the population as the Negro and the Puerto Rican is very much higher than that of the white. . . . The problem is to determine how we can apply this fundamental principle of working through the mores of these groups to motivate them."[26]

2. *Related to Public Reaction.* Public service and community action programs build up a vested interest not only among program staff, but also among the recipients of the services themselves and often the community at large. Once the public has become accustomed to a program, it is likely to resist having it curtailed—even if an evaluation study shows the program to be ineffective. Many health, education, and welfare programs continue to exist despite professional knowledge of their uselessness because of public demand. One might paraphrase George Bernard Shaw by warning that "the public must be given what it needs, or it will learn to like what it gets."

Anthropologists have been particularly concerned with the need to take the state of community readiness into account before introducing new programs or changes into old, established programs. Saunders and Samora point this out in relation to a medical care program among the Spanish-Americans in the Southwest. "In the field of health, as in other fields, action programs cutting across cultural or subcultural lines must, if they are to be accepted, conform to the existing perceptions, beliefs, attitudes, and practices of the group they are to affect. Furthermore, if such programs are to have any chance of continuing after the initial organizing impetus is withdrawn, they must permit the pursuit of culturally meaningful goals through culturally acceptable means."[27]

Some of the problems encountered by practitioners in implementing the recommended changes of a program evaluation stem from their failure to recognize what Polgar has termed "four cultural fallacies": First, the "fallacy of the empty vessel"—the tendency to act as if no health measures or "popular" health culture existed prior to the proposed change and to fail to build a new approach upon the positive features of already existing practices. Second, the "fallacy of the separate capsule" —the tendency to determine the limits of program change based upon one's own beliefs and practices. Third, the "fallacy of the single pyramid"

—the tendency to assume homogeneity of the public especially within the artificially created boundaries of one's own administrative organization. Fourth, the "fallacy of the interchangeable faces"—the tendency to ignore important individual differences and person-to-person relationships especially among subcultural groups. Polgar documents each of these fallacies with many illustrations of how their disregard by public health workers interfered with their ability to implement program change.[28]

The social researcher performing an evaluation of public service and community action programs is in a position, as a social scientist, to be particularly aware of the organizational and public pressures which have to be taken into account in translating the results of an evaluation study into action. In addition to his technical competence as a research worker, he brings a knowledge of organizational and community structure and function which has direct relevance to the implementation of program change. His substantive contribution in this area can be as great, and perhaps even more telling, than his methodological skills in conducting evaluative research.

N O T E S   T O   C H A P T E R   I X

1. Sjoberg, Gideon, "Research Methodology: A Sociology of Knowledge Perspective." Paper presented to the Sociological Research Association, Chicago, August 31, 1965.
2. Suchman, Edward A., "The Principles of Research Design," in Doby, John T., and others, *An Introduction to Social Research.* The Stackpole Co., Harrisburg, Pa., 1954, p. 254.
3. James, George, "Research by Local Health Departments—Problems, Methods, Results," *American Journal of Public Health,* vol. 48, March, 1958, p. 354.
4. Paul, Benjamin D., William A. Gamson, S. Stephen Kegeles, editors, *Trigger for Community Conflict: The Case of Fluoridation,* Journal of Social Issues, vol. 17, no. 4, 1961. (Entire issue.) These studies illustrate the many additional social factors that enter into any public action decision besides the evaluative findings.
5. Blum, Hendrik L., and Alvin R. Leonard, *Public Administration: A Public Health Viewpoint.* Macmillan Co., New York, 1963, p. 316.
6. *Ibid.,* p. 315.
7. Cottrell, Leonard S., Jr., and Eleanor B. Sheldon, "Problems of Collaboration Between Social Scientists and the Practicing Professions," *The Annals of the American Academy of Political and Social Science,* vol. 346,

March, 1963, pp. 126–137. See also Suchman, Edward A., *Sociology and the Field of Public Health,* Russell Sage Foundation, New York, 1963, pp. 155–174.

8. Wright, Charles R., and Herbert H. Hyman, "The Evaluators," in Hammond, Phillip E., editor, *Sociologists at Work.* Basic Books, New York, 1964, p. 123.

9. Bergen, Bernard J. "Professional Communities and the Evaluation of Demonstration Projects in Community Mental Health," *American Journal of Public Health,* vol. 55, July, 1965, p. 1058.

10. Herzog, Elizabeth, *Some Guide Lines for Evaluative Research.* U.S. Department of Health, Education, and Welfare, Children's Bureau, Washington, 1959, p. 88.

11. Metzner, Charles A., and Gerald Gurin, *Personal Response and Social Organization in a Health Campaign.* University of Michigan, Bureau of Public Health Economics, Research Series No. 9, Ann Arbor, 1960, p. 8.

12. Resistance to "outside" evaluation is reported by Metzner and Gurin as follows: "Any attempt at evaluation, particularly from the outside, may well be conceived as a threat. It is an examination and report concerning how well people are doing. Very few people are so secure, or unaware of their own deficiencies, that an unknown with a notebook will arouse no anxieties. This is particularly true if the evaluators are not responding to local desire, but are brought in from above, and the purposes and relations are unclear." *Ibid.,* p. 8.

13. This need for a cooperative relationship has been noted by Dressell and Mayhew in relation to educational evaluation. They state: "Approached in this way, it was apparent that evaluation must be a cooperative enterprise—cooperative in many ways for many reasons. The more complex behavioral outcomes require cooperation between teachers and evaluators in developing procedures and in collecting evidence—cooperation of administrators, personnel workers, and of the students themselves—if time is to be found, if a broad range of evidence is to be collected, and if students are to be properly motivated. Student motivation through cooperation is particularly important. Similarly, evaluation done by evaluators without the full cooperation of teachers is apt to be misunderstood and even rejected." Dressell, Paul L., and Lewis B. Mayhew, *General Education: Exploration in Evaluation.* American Council on Education, Washington, 1954, pp. 23–24.

14. As reported by Bernard J. Bergen, *op. cit.,* p. 1057.

15. MacMahon, Brian, Thomas F. Pugh, and George B. Hutchison, "Principles in the Evaluation of Community Health Programs," *American Journal of Public Health,* vol. 51, July, 1961, p. 964.

16. *Organizational Study on Programme Analysis and Evaluation.* World Health Organization, Geneva, Switzerland, January 8, 1954, p. 37.

17. Merton, Robert K., "The Role of Applied Social Science in the Formation of Policy," *Philosophy of Science,* vol. 16, July, 1949, p. 172.

18. As reported in *Proceedings of an Invitational Conference on Social Research in the Development of Health and Welfare Agency Programs.* State Charities Aid Association, New York, April, 1961, p. 62.

19. Clausen, John, "Reality Testing: Theory and Experience in Research Formulation," in *Report of Technical Assistance Project Workshop on Research in Social Problem Areas,* San Diego, Calif., April 15–18, 1962, p. 56.

20. Meyer, Henry J., and Edgar F. Borgatta, "Evaluating a Rehabilitation Program for Post-Hospital Mental Patients," *Public Health Reports,* vol. 73, July, 1958, p. 650. See also, by the same authors, "Paradoxes in Evaluating Mental Health Programmes," *International Journal of Social Psychiatry,* Winter, 1959, p. 136.

21. For a good discussion of this problem, see Selltiz, Claire, and others, *Research Methods in Social Relations,* Holt, Rinehart and Winston, New York, 1965, pp. 455–477. Hyman also presents an extensive discussion of the relation between research and social policy; see Hyman, Herbert H., *Survey Design and Analysis,* The Free Press, Glencoe, Ill., 1955.

22. Dressel, Paul L., and Lewis B. Mayhew, *op. cit.,* p. 25.

23. Merton, Robert K., *op. cit.,* pp. 175–177.

24. Dressel, Paul L., and Lewis B. Mayhew, *op. cit.,* p. 29.

25. *Proceedings of an Invitational Conference on Social Research in the Development of Health and Welfare Agency Programs, op. cit.,* p. 19. This report offers an excellent discussion of the general problems of collaboration between researchers and administrators.

26. *Ibid.,* p. 52.

27. Saunders, Lyle, and Julian Samora, "A Medical Care Program in a Colorado County," in Paul, Benjamin D., editor, *Health, Culture, and Community.* Russell Sage Foundation, New York, 1955, pp. 377–400. The specific details of this experience are worth quoting:

> The Brazos County Health Association, along with the New Mexico health cooperative and numerous other health programs in the Southwest, satisfied neither of these conditions. Many aspects of the Association's program were at variance with traditional Spanish-American ways of dealing with sickness. It was an imposed program; it violated established leadership practices; it ran counter to the accepted method of dealing with sickness on an individual basis. A whole set of seemingly irrelevant actions—joining an organization, attending meetings, paying fees, voting, and the like—became attached to the treatment of sickness and became a condition of participation in the new arrangement. While the Association's major goal, better health for Brazos County, was probably acceptable in the abstract, such related subgoals as the maintenance of an organization, the development of preventive procedures and attitudes, and the building of a health center were not meaningful or important to many local people. (p. 398)

28. Polgar, Steven, "Health Action in Cross-Cultural Perspectives," in Freeman, Howard, Sol Levine, and Leo G. Reeder, editors, *Handbook of Medical Sociology.* Prentice-Hall, Inc., Englewood Cliffs, N.J., 1963, pp. 411–414.

CHAPTER X

The Social Experiment and the Future
of Evaluative Research

The study of induced social change has long been an area of major interest among social scientists. Economists have attempted to regulate the "ups and downs" of economic systems through various fiscal and monetary controls. Sociologists may be found in almost all types of public and private organizations devoted to meeting a wide variety of social problems. Psychologists have attempted to influence human behavior in almost all social institutions from the school to the market place. Anthropologists have applied their knowledge of cultural factors to overcome resistance to innovation in the underdeveloped parts of the world. Political scientists are increasingly becoming concerned with the more practical aspects of politics and government.

As these social scientists have moved out of the familiar and more or less comfortable environment of academia into a strange and anxiety-provoking world of action and policy-making, they have had to face two major problems. How could they translate their fund of knowledge into decisions about program operation in such a way as to feel reasonably sure that their recommendations for action were correct, and how could they develop from these experiences more general rules which could gradually accumulate into a body of principles for social action and policy-making? On the one hand, they wanted to apply what they knew, while, on the other hand, they wished to learn from what they applied.

This problem of "exchange" between basic and applied research is not a new one for the social scientist and is directly applicable to the relationship between nonevaluative and evaluative research. As analyzed by Merton, "Since applied research is conceived as a basis for action and since action must always occur in a *concrete* situation and not under abstractly envisaged conditions, the applied researcher is continuously engaged, *nolens volens*, in testing the assumptions contained in basic theory. This is perhaps a key function of applied research."[1]

We have already discussed this problem in the chapters on methodology and concluded that evaluative research provides the possibility for the development of a new form of "social experimentation" as a model for research on public service and social action programs. Here we would like to expand briefly on this prospect as offering the greatest challenge for evaluation research in the future. In this connection, we have stated elsewhere:

> To some extent evaluative research may offer a bridge between "pure" and "applied" research. Evaluation may be viewed as a field test of the validity of cause-effect hypotheses in basic science whether these be in the field of biology (i.e., medicine) or sociology (i.e., social work). Action programs in any professional field should be based upon the best available scientific knowledge and theory of that field. As such, evaluations of the success or failure of these programs are intimately tied into the proof or disproof of such knowledge. Since such a knowledge base is the foundation of any action program, the evaluative research worker who approaches his task in the spirit of testing some theoretical proposition rather than a set of administrative practices will in the long run make the most significant contribution to program development.[2]

AN EVALUATION MODEL FOR THE SOCIAL EXPERIMENT

Renewed interest in evaluative research as the study of the desirable and undesirable consequences of planned social change has produced a new awareness of the "experimental" foundations of social research. While the idea of the social experiment has permeated sociology since the days of Comte, actual attempts to utilize the experimental method for social research have been few and far between—and, for the most part, largely unsuccessful.

In an effort to stimulate interest in the use of the experimental method in social research, first Greenwood[3] and then Chapin[4] offered a conceptual and methodological analysis of the experimental approach which considerably broadened the logical model to include the longitudinal and "ex-post-facto" social survey. Greenwood argued, "Perfect control, while it is something to aim at, is almost never possible. The experimenter must therefore always aspire after the maximum control that circumstances will permit. As in everything else, so here, gradations exist. There are good approximations to the ideal experiment and there are poor ones."[5]

Chapin accepted this attempt at a realistic compromise and brought together nine examples of social experimentation in a critique which he characterized as "the crude beginnings of efforts to observe, under conditions of control by matching, what really happened to people when such trial and error experiments, taking the form of programs of social treatment or social reform, were used to influence them. It was my purpose to show that the systematic study of social action is necessary if we are to appraise objectively the results often claimed for such programs."[6]

This broad approach to experimental social research, in effect, acknowledges the limited applicability of the classical controlled experiment to social action programs and suggests that studies designed to evaluate such programs make use instead of existing models of social research, particularly the prospective or panel design and the retrospective or "ex-post-facto" survey. While there are certain administrative restrictions imposed by the fact that one must usually deal with ongoing programs, the logical model for both conceptual analysis and methodological design remains largely the same for nonevaluative and evaluative research.[7]

This inherent similarity points the way toward a more productive use of evaluative research, both to test the effectiveness of social action programs and to advance behavioral science knowledge. It is our conviction that the future success of evaluation research will depend, to a large measure, upon its ability to adapt existing models of social research to field studies of action programs. Such success offers hope for the growth of a new form of "social experiment" which will provide a valuable opportunity for both the expansion and utilization of social knowledge.

EVALUATION AND SOCIAL CAUSATION

One of the most useful models for the theoretical analysis of and empirical research upon social phenomena is derived from the concept of causality as a chain or nexus of events related along a time dimension. As formulated by Chapin, "Cause and effect, or causality as a system of ideas, is an explanation of successive events by a set of assumed antecedent-consequent relationships. . . . The concept of cause and effect . . . is used as a shorthand device to represent a kind of association between factors in time sequence which has a determinable probability of occurrence."[8] In this chapter, we will take one of the major components of this approach, namely, the intervening variable, and demonstrate its applicability to evaluative research.

This model of intervening variable analysis has been discussed in the chapters on methodology as a logical procedure for the determination of independent-dependent relationships and the further analysis of these relationships in terms of "control" variables. In general, the process begins with the establishment of some antecedent-consequent relationship which is then tested for validity or "spuriousness" in terms of some intervening variable which may or may not destroy or modify the original relationship. While both the logical and statistical operations of this model are open to some debate, it does constitute at the moment one of the most common forms of social research.

In applying this model to evaluative research, we immediately note a highly significant change in the manner in which the basic independent-dependent hypothesis is formulated. The nonevaluative hypothesis usually takes the form of "the more A (independent variable), the more B (dependent variable)"; in evaluative research this becomes "changing variable A will produce a desired change in variable B." The process whereby A is changed becomes the program activity to be evaluated, while the changes achieved in B become the program objectives to be attained. Thus, the evaluative hypothesis might now read, "Activities A, B, C . . . N will attain objectives X, Y, Z . . . N."

The first basic step of evaluative research, then, will be to show the extent to which specified activities do attain defined objectives. For this reason, we have argued that two crucial problems in evaluation become: (1) the isolation of program elements designed to produce change (tantamount to the definition and isolation of one's independent or experimental "stimulus" variable); and (2) the formulation of criteria for the desired change or objectives (tantamount to the specification and measurement of one's dependent variable or experimental "effect").

For many purely operational programs, it may be sufficient to conclude one's evaluation with the answer to this first question—the program works or it does not work. However, just as the determination of the existence of a relationship between an independent and dependent variable is only the jumping-off point for nonevaluative research, so, in evaluative research also, the next questions become, "Given a relationship between activity A and objective B, (1) How do we know objective B was really attained because of activity A? (2) What preconditions were necessary for initiating activity A and helpful in attaining objective B? (3) How and why did activity A result in objectives B—what intervening factors led to or modified the effects obtained? (4) What will be the consequences of having attained objective B—will there be any negative or "boomerang" effects?" The similarity between these four questions and those usually posed in relation to the analytic model of nonevaluative research is not purely coincidental.

We may view a social action program as a form of intervention which attempts to prevent certain undesirable effects or consequences from developing by a deliberate attack upon causes or antecedent events. Chapin indicated this underlying rationale when he observed: "Programs to prevent the recurrence of social ills always rest upon the assumption that social cause and effect sequences are known, whether or not this assumption is implicit or explicitly stated in the program."[9] Employing the analytic model of intervening variable analysis, we may conceptualize the intervention process largely as one attempting to alter the causal nexus between the independent and dependent variable through manipulation of the intervening variables by means of which the cause leads to the effect, or which modify or condition the effect.

Three such major independent-intervening-dependent subgroupings exist: (1) the relationship between the precondition and causal variables, (2) the relationship between the cause-and-effect variables, and (3) the relationship between the effect and the consequence variables. Each of these pairs of relationships may be analyzed in terms of the intervening variables occurring between the two, and each pair offers a conceptually different possibility of prevention through intervention with the intervening variable. These three possibilities may be diagrammed as follows:

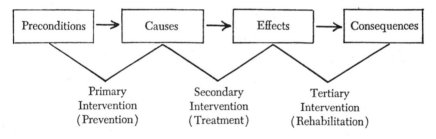

APPLICATIONS OF INTERVENING VARIABLE MODEL

We may briefly note some significant differences in the three major areas of social action programs today—health, education, and welfare—in regard to both traditional and future activities. Traditionally, the field of health or medicine is largely concerned with the treatment process; physicians provide medical care to patients who have already developed the causes of illness and the objective of medical "intervention" is to prevent the full effects of the disease—death or disability—from developing. Thus, the current emphasis of medical programs is predominantly upon secondary prevention. However, with the increasing importance of the chronic, degenerative diseases (such as heart disease or diabetes) where medical treatment offers little promise of any cure, the shift of future programs is toward tertiary prevention or rehabilitation of the patient who has already suffered the effects of the disease or disability, and to a lesser degree, upon primary prevention to decrease the probability of the development of causes of the degenerative disease.

In regard to education, the traditional emphasis has also been upon secondary intervention, the major objective of educational programs being to decrease the negative effects of a lack of education by intervening with teaching and training programs aimed at preventing the effects of ignorance or a lack of skill. Today, there is increasing emphasis, on the one hand, upon tertiary intervention designed to reduce the consequences of a lack of education by providing adult education and training programs, and, on the other hand, upon primary intervention with preschool programs aimed at overcoming some of the preconditions of the culturally disadvantaged which interfere with their exposure to the desirable effects of educational intervention.

Finally, in the field of welfare, we find social work overwhelmingly concerned with meeting the *consequences* of poverty and misfortune in what might be called tertiary intervention or the amelioration of social ills that have already occurred. Here, too, however, traditional programs are being increasingly challenged by those progressives in the field of social work who argue that what is needed is a greater emphasis upon primary intervention, or an attack by social work upon the preconditions of social problems, and secondary intervention or social work intervention to prevent existing social conditions from developing their full negative effects.

This characterization of the three fields of health, education, and welfare would tend to support the general proposition that social action programs are needed at all three stages of primary, secondary, and tertiary intervention. In a conceptual sense, this principle of social action supports the usual formulation of a continuous causal sequence containing an unlimited number of independent-intervening-dependent relationships occurring at any stage between preconditions and consequences. Intervention may take place at any point of time along this sequence, dictated probably by a combination of social values as to which dependent effects are most worth preventing and action potentials as to which independent and intervening variables are most susceptible to and acceptable for manipulation.

The application of the proposed model of intervening variable analysis to evaluative research has many significant conceptual and methodological implications. In this concluding chapter, we mention some of these briefly as stimuli to further thought.

1. The prospective or longitudinal panel design comes closest to satisfying the methodological requirements of the experimental model and offers the greatest promise for evaluative research. This is largely because evaluation over time provides a technique for making "before" and "after" measurements and for placing the independent, intervening, and dependent variables in proper sequence. However, evaluative research can and does utilize the ex-post-facto survey design and the clinical case study method, although the same limitations of interpretation and "proof" prevail as for nonevaluative research.

2. Just as "complete" explanation is never possible in nonevaluative research because of the multiplicity of intervening variables with relationships being given in terms of probabilities, so absolute program effectiveness is also impossible and success becomes a matter of degree. Related to this multiplicity of factors is the special need in evaluative research to take into account the "boomerang" or negative side effects which are the almost inevitable consequences of any social action program.

3. The intervening variables in evaluative research may be conceived as a series of "steps" ranging from immediate to intermediate and ultimate objectives. These steps usually comprise a continuous series of events which, for evaluation purposes, may be subdivided into a hierarchy of subgoals, each of which may be viewed as the successful result of a preceding goal and, in turn, as a precondition for the next higher goal. Intervention aimed at higher levels of objectives will subsume the validity of lower-order objectives and will have greater generalizability. Effectiveness at the top of the scale generally subsumes effectiveness at lower levels.

4. A major problem in the definition of the intervening variable in evaluative research is the extent to which this variable constitutes an operational index of some broader concept or principle of intervention or a program activity with operational validity of its own. In nonevalu-

ative research, the concept is of major importance and the operational index has little inherent importance. In evaluative research, these operational indices may be significant in and of themselves as specific program activities designed to produce the desired effect.

5. We may conceive of the "intervention power" of a social action variable in the same sense as we talk about the "explanatory power" of an intervening variable in nonevaluative research. In "explanation," we hold the test variable constant in an attempt to destroy or alter the independent-dependent relationship. In "intervention," we control or manipulate the action variable in an attempt to change the ability of the independent variable to produce the dependent effect.

6. The "validity" of the intervening variable being manipulated is crucial to the success of the action program. Changing a "spurious" intervening variable will not produce the desired effects. In some cases this has been referred to as the "Hawthorne Effect," although it is important to distinguish whether such effects are really "spurious" or an inherent aspect of the action program. In this sense the "placebo" in medical evaluation studies should not be confused with nontreatment.

7. In nonevaluative research, the independent variable is usually some demographic characteristic, while the dependent variable represents behavior or action. The intervening variable tends to become some "dispositional" factor (that is, attitude or value) which "underlies" the demographic factor. These "dispositional" factors are most often the target of social action programs, since little can be done to change the demographic characteristics and these intervening variables are usually viewed as "accounting for" the demographic differences. Again, this approach supports our contention that intervention is largely a matter of manipulating the intervening variable.

CONCLUSION

The evaluation of social action programs approached in terms of a conceptual and methodological model of evaluative research as discussed above can make a major contribution both to social action and to social knowledge. Social research techniques for the collection and analysis of data are fully applicable to the study of planned social change—which is basically what is involved in current national and international social action programs. These programs constitute social "experiments" worthy of the serious attention of social theorists and methodologists. They hold the promise of the successful development of an "experimental" sociology in which the intervening variable so prominent in nonevaluative research becomes in actuality a form of social intervention.

In its broadest framework, then, evaluative research becomes the study of planned programs for producing social change through social experiments. These experiments test the validity of the hypothesis that the action program has within it elements that will affect certain "causal" factors in the development of the desired objective. Thus, we try to reduce disease, increase education, or improve the social welfare by planning programs which we have some theoretical reason for believing will alter the factors or processes that influence disease, education, or welfare. What we evaluate is the action hypothesis that defined program activities will achieve specified, desired objectives through their ability to influence those intervening processes that affect the occurrence of these objectives.

Thus, for example, in public health, we would try to evaluate the ability of a mass x-ray program to lower the mortality of tuberculosis because we hypothesize that such a program will lead to earlier case-finding which we have reason to believe will result in earlier treatment and a decrease in mortality. In education, we might try to reduce school dropouts by a program of occupational guidance because such a program would make the student more aware of future job opportunities and such awareness is an important factor in educational motivation. In welfare, a program of sheltered workshops might be established to reduce unemployment among the physically handicapped because we hypothesize that such workshops provide the kind of occupational training that helps the handicapped person find and hold jobs. In each of these examples, the evaluation study tests some hypothesis that activity A will attain objective B because it is able to influence process C which affects the occurrence of this objective. An understanding of all three factors—program, objective, and intervening process—is essential to the conduct of evaluative research.

NOTES TO CHAPTER X

1. Merton, Robert K., "The Role of Applied Social Science in the Formation of Policy," *Philosophy of Science*, vol. 16, July, 1949, p. 179.
2. Suchman, Edward A., "Principles and Practice of Evaluative Research,"

in Doby, John, and others, *An Introduction to Social Research.* Revised
edition. Appleton-Century-Crofts, New York, 1967.

3. Greenwood, Ernest, *Experimental Sociology.* King's Crown Press, New
   York, 1945.
4. Chapin, F. Stuart, *Experimental Designs in Sociological Research.* Harper
   and Bros., New York, 1947 (rev., 1955).
5. Greenwood, Ernest, *op. cit.*, p. 29.
6. Chapin, F. Stuart, *op. cit.*, p. 279. According to Chapin, "Social experimentation . . . seeks to achieve some *desired change* in social relations.
   As such, it may be distinguished from experimental designs which seek
   to obtain observations of social relations under conditions of control." (p.
   26)
7. Suchman, Edward A., "A Model for Research and Evaluation on Rehabilitation," in Sussman, Marvin, editor, *Sociology and Rehabilitation.* Vocational
   Rehabilitation Administration, Washington, 1966, pp. 52–70.
8. Chapin, F. Stuart, *op. cit.*, pp. 52–53.
9. *Ibid.*, p. viii.

INDEX

INDEX

Abuses of evaluation studies, 143–145
Ackoff, Russell L., 66, 73, 111, 113, 149
Adequacy of performance, evaluation of,
    63–64
    See also Performance
Administration of evaluation studies:
    Conflicts with evaluator, 155–161
    Defining objectives, 158–161
    Limitations, 21–22
    Problems enumerated, 151–152
    Relation to public, 152–153, 165–166
    Resources for research, 153–155
    Utilization of research, 162–166
    See also Program administration
Administrative science, 132
    See also Program administration
Anderson, Otis L., 29, 31, 46, 149
Andrews, Frank M., 113
Appraisal forms. *See* Community evalua-
    tion guides
Arbona, Guillermo, 146, 149
Arnoff, E. Leonard, 149
Arnold, Francis A., Jr., 50
Assumptions. *See* Validity assumptions;
    Value assumptions
Attitudes of public toward public service
    programs, 4, 152–153, 165–166

Ballard, Robert G., 109, 114
Barrabee, Edna L., 130
Barton, Allen H., 9, 113
Baumgartner, Leona, 26
Beecher, H. K., 111
Benne, Kenneth B., 47
Bennis, Warren G., 47
Berelson, Bernard, 112, 147, 150
Bergen, Bernard J., 156, 167
Bias:
    In reliability, 166
    In self-evaluation, 157
    In validity, 122
Bigman, Stanley K., 30, 46, 64, 73, 127,
    129, 130
Blalock, Hubert M., Jr., 114
Blau, Peter M., 107, 114
Blenckner, M., 113
Bloch, Donald A., 86, 90
Blood, J. W., 148
Blum, Hendrik L., 140, 148–149, 154,
    166
"Boomerang" effects. *See* Negative
    effects

Boran, Behice, 90
Borgatta, Edgar F., 29, 45, 50, 100, 104,
    105, 107, 112, 113, 138, 143, 144,
    147, 148, 149, 150, 162, 168
Breedlove, J. L., 9
Brim, Orville G., Jr., 9
Brogden, Hubert E., 123, 130
Burruss, Genette, 48

Campbell, D. T., 93, 111
Carlson, R. O., 127, 131
Case study evaluation, 93–94
Categories of evaluation, 60–68
Cattell, Raymond B., 108, 114
Causal process, 83–88, 171–176
Chadwick, John Howard, 13
Chain of objectives. *See* Objectives
Chapin, Charles V., 14, 24
Chapin, F. Stuart, 112, 114, 170, 171,
    173, 178
Chein, Isadore, 49
Chin, Robert, 47
Churchman, C. West, 89, 149
Ciocco, Antonio, 19, 24, 25, 49, 124, 130
Clark, E. Gurney, 118, 130
Clausen, John, 161, 168
Cochran, William G., 103, 111, 112, 113
Community evaluation guides:
    Development of, 14
    Shortcomings of, 14–18
Community services. *See* Public service
    programs and agencies
Concepts of evaluation, 28–29
Conflicts between administrators and
    evaluators, 35–37, 155–161
Control group design, 95–96
Control groups, selecting and sampling,
    102–105
Cooperation of public. *See* Public atti-
    tudes toward public service pro-
    grams
Cornfield, Jerome, 85, 90, 111
Cost of public service programs, 145–
    146, 153
Cottrell, Leonard S., Jr., vii–viii,
    166–167
Cox, G. M., 112
Criswell, John W., 148
Criteria:
    Determination of, 123
    Of success, 54, 60–71, 115–128
    Of validity, 108–110

181